What Happens After We Die?

Douglas Jacoby

What Happens After We Die?
© 2013 by Douglas Jacoby

Printed in the United States of America.

ISBN: 978-0-9849087-5-2

Unless otherwise indicated, all Scripture references are from the *Holy Bible, New International Version*, copyright ©1973, 1978, 1984, 2011 by Biblica, Inc. Used by permission. All rights reserved worldwide.

Verses marked NLT are taken from the *Holy Bible, New Living Translation*, copyright ©1996. Used by permission of Tyndale House Publishers, Inc. Wheaton, IL 60189 USA. All rights reserved.

Verses marked NKJV are taken from the *New King James Version*, Copyright ©1982 by Thomas Nelson, Inc. Used by permission. All rights reserved.

Verses marked NASB are taken from the *New American Standard Bible®*, Copyright © 1960, 1962, 1963, 1968, 1971, 1972, 1973, 1975, 1977, 1995 by The Lockman Foundation. Used by permission.

Scripture quotations marked HCSB are taken from the *Holman Christian Standard Bible®*, used by permission HCSB ©1999,2000,2002,2003,2009. Holman Bible Publishers.

About the author: Dr. Douglas Jacoby graduated in 1980 from Duke University (history). In 1982, he received an MTS from Harvard (New Testament), followed by three years of post-graduate study at Kings College London. He took his doctorate in 1999 from Drew University (Christian education). In addition to serving as Adjunct Professor at Lincoln Christian University, Douglas has had an international teaching impact for several decades, preaching in 500 cities in over 100 nations around the globe. For additional information about his ministry, visit www.DouglasJacoby.com and www.jacobypremium.com.

Cover and book interior design: Toney C. Mulhollan

ILLUMINATION **IP**
PUBLISHERS

6010 Pinecreek Ridge Court, Spring, Texas 77379-2513 • www.ipibooks.com

Contents

Acknowledgements

It is because of Toney Mulhollan, my publisher, that this book came to be. Few humans I know exhibit his level of industry, positive attitude, and stamina. His vision for the project supplied impetus and direction. Likewise, Toney and I together are grateful to three remarkable women who undertook the hard work of transcribing the original *What Happens?* series, softening and smoothing the rough document that resulted, and editing and proofing the emerging book. Sterna Müller, Elizabeth Thompson, and Amy Morgan, you have been a joy. Thank you.

Chapter 1

After Death: Have We Got It All Wrong?

What happens after we die? There are few questions more universal than this. We all want to know what happens when we die. No matter our religion, culture, or social status, no one is indifferent about death.

But exactly what happens the instant we die? Is there a second chance for those who did not turn to the Lord during their earthly lives? Do we become angels, floating up in the clouds, or ghosts, restlessly roaming the earth? Do we go down a tunnel of light? Are people even conscious of what happens between death and Judgment Day, or does our soul simply go to sleep? Do we go straight to heaven, and keep an eye on our friends and family still on earth?

When I was five or six years old, I was given a book called *The Littlest Angel*. In the book, a child dies and becomes an angel, and that idea is embraced by many people who claim to be Christians. And even though Christians hold different opinions about some details about the afterlife, we find virtual unanimity on one conviction: Nearly everyone agrees that when Christians die, they go straight to heaven.

5

I often walk through a cemetery during my morning prayer times, and most of the headstones proclaim that the departed are now in heaven, illustrating the predominant Christian belief in immediate departure. When you go to a funeral, you never hear the preacher say, "Well, unfortunately this person did not put the Lord first and he is in a hot place right now." But you also never hear the preacher claim that the person has gone to the "intermediate place." No—almost without fail, we are told that our deceased friend or relative is already looking down on us from heaven.

But in spite of this idea's popularity, I believe it is in error. If that statement sounds like heresy, stay with me through the end of this chapter. Let's consider a brief passage in Luke, which brings up a number of questions about what happens after death. In Luke 23:43, Jesus makes a promise to the thief on the cross: "Today you will be with me in paradise." In Scripture, the most literal interpretation is not always the correct one, but very often it is. So if we take Jesus' words at face value, we would expect Jesus and the thief to meet up later that day in paradise! Since most Christians equate paradise with heaven, they would interpret this statement to mean that Jesus and the thief went to heaven together that day.

But when we read John 20:17, we encounter a problem. Here the resurrected Jesus tells Mary, "Do not hold on to me, for I have not yet returned to the Father." Jesus is telling Mary that he hasn't gone to be with his Father in heaven yet. But if heaven and paradise are the same place, then Jesus has contradicted himself! How could the thief join Jesus in paradise if Jesus had not yet ascended to the Father?

Many people explain this away by saying, "Well today just means a physiological instant. What Jesus really meant was that the next thing the thief knew, he would be in heaven." Again, they assume that paradise is the same thing as heaven. But why not take Jesus at his word? Why not understand his promise to the thief in the simplest way possible? What if Jesus really meant that on that very day, as we mortals reckon time, the thief would be with Jesus in paradise? This experience would obviously be a good one, and it was also something of which the thief would be conscious.

So which one was it? Would the thief go to be with Jesus that same day? Or would they meet in his next moment of consciousness? Or would it be thousands of years later?

Assuming that Jesus meant what he said, and planned to meet the penitent thief that same day, then where did Jesus plan on meeting him? What is paradise? And is the traditional view of what happens after death in accord with what the Scriptures teach? These questions, and many more, will be addressed and answered in this book.

As we will see, the early Christians taught that, ten days before Pentecost, or some forty days after Easter Sunday, Jesus was standing on the Mount of Olives in the area of Bethany, and he ascended to heaven in bodily form. In other words, Jesus did not go to heaven until the ascension. We will examine proofs of this position throughout the New Testament and the early Christian writings.

But here in the first chapter, we will begin by exploring our common understanding of what happens after we die.

After Death: Have We Got It All Wrong?

The truth about life after death is quite different from the popular teachings we hear in religious circles today–not just at funerals, but also in churches, where the topic is frequently discussed from the pulpit. The commonly perceived scenario is that, on death, if we are right with the Lord, we go immediately to heaven; or if we are not right with the Lord, we go immediately to the lake of fire, or hell. This book will demonstrate that the New Testament teaching on this subject is different, and it is actually clearly laid out in the following sequence:

After death, we descend into Hades–the intermediate state of the dead, sometimes called the underworld. Only when Jesus returns will we be resurrected, and after the Judgment Day we will go to our final destiny: either the lake of fire or heaven.

The sequence then is as follows: Death–Hades–The Second Coming–The Resurrection–Judgment–Final Destiny. This teaching is not only found in the New Testament, but is also revealed in early Christian literature. But starting in the third and fourth centuries, it began to undergo modification, and by the year AD 400 or 500, the concept of Hades as the intermediate place of the dead had been transformed into the concept of purgatory.

More than a thousand years later, the Protestant Reformation began, and in the 1500s, many of the medieval doctrines were dismissed or reevaluated. While it was good to reconsider the traditional ideas, the traditional ideas were not all wrong! The early reformers were working to return to the teachings of the New Testament and the early church. Martin Luther (1483-1546) and John Calvin (1509-1564) are usually considered the foremost reformers of the Reformation in that early period.

The Catholics taught that unless you are exceptionally good (in which case you go straight to heaven), or exceptionally bad (in which case you go straight to hell), you go to purgatory after you die. Most people would go to purgatory, a place of cleansing where they would receive the punishment necessary to cleanse them of their sins. After someone had been in purgatory and had suffered long enough, they would be released and promoted, or upgraded.

Both Martin Luther and John Calvin tried to reclaim the doctrine of the intermediate state of the dead, yet in time, they succumbed to pressure and gave up their quest. They (and their followers, known as Protestants) rejected the teaching of purgatory but failed to embrace the concept of Hades. In just a few years, they transitioned to a hybrid doctrine that combined biblical doctrine with medieval teachings. Protestants began to teach that after death people did not go to purgatory, but went straight to heaven. They omitted the intermediate state altogether.

This was an unfortunate overreaction. But church history itself, in many ways, can be understood as a long history of overreactions. It is tempting for us to say, "If we had lived in their day, we would not have made their mistakes. We would have handled things better." It is easy to say that, and yet we are all weak and prone to overreaction.

To understand the New Testament teaching on this

subject, we have to begin by understanding New Testament cosmology, which is the study of the cosmos or the universe. When we talk about cosmology from the modern perspective, we are referring to not just our solar system and its galaxy, but all the galaxies in the whole universe. In the ancient world, people had a different view, and they held a tripartite concept of cosmology, meaning there were three parts to the cosmos.

With their three parts of the cosmos, they believed that when anyone went up from the earth, they would go right to heaven. Before we are tempted to laugh at that belief, think about this: If you were leaving our planet, any direction you were going would be going up, wouldn't it? And that has nothing to do with your view of the shape of the earth! You may be surprised to learn that many ancients believed the earth was round or spherical, while others thought it was a disc. But regardless, the only way "out" was "up"—so of course heaven must be above the earth. But the ancients did not only believe in a heaven, they also believed in an underworld. They conceived of the place of death, called Hades, as being under the earth.

Ephesians 4:8-10 is a familiar passage that we often skip over when preaching:

> This is why it says:
>> "When he ascended on high,
>>> he led captives in his train
>>> and gave gifts to men."
>
> (What does "he ascended" mean except that he also descended

to the lower, earthly regions? He who descended is the very one who ascended higher than all the heavens, in order to fill the whole universe.)

I used to look at this and interpret the middle verse (verse 9) logically: I thought it meant that if he ascended, then he also descended; that is, if he went up (to heaven), then he must have been down before (when he was on earth). I took the lower earthly regions to mean the earth itself, and that is the view some commentators have followed, though not traditionally. I argued against what I call the symmetrical view—that if he had gone up, then he must, from the same starting place (earth), also have gone down (into Hades). But actually, the New Testament does talk about the descent of Christ into the underworld (i.e. 1 Peter 3:18-20).

Let's read that verse again with the other possibility in mind. This time let's look at the New American Standard Version, which in my opinion is translated more accurately:

Now this expression, "He ascended," what does it mean except that He also had descended into the lower parts of the earth? He who descended is Himself also He who ascended far above all the heavens, so that He might fill all things. (Ephesians 4:9-10)

"Filling all things" encompasses all three levels of the ancient understanding of the cosmos: heaven, earth, and Hades (the place of the dead).

This understanding would also make sense of another passage that is even more familiar to many of us: Philippians

2:9-11, which describes the emptying and then exaltation of Christ:

> Therefore God exalted him to the highest place
>   and gave him the name that is above every name,
> that at the name of Jesus every knee should bow,
>   in heaven and on earth and under the earth,
> and every tongue confess that Jesus Christ is Lord,
>   to the glory of God the Father.

Once again, we find the tripartite universe.

Now that we have discussed cosmology, the ancient concept of the three-part cosmos, we are prepared to explore some of the most important ideas in both testaments about death and what follows. We will need to examine several key terms that Bible writers used to define and describe the afterlife.

Hades

In the Old Testament, the Hebrew word *Sheol* is found sixty-seven times. *Sheol* is equivalent to the New Testament word *Hades*, which appears many times as well. Sheol is the place of the dead, and it is a place of darkness, rest and waiting. All people go there, both the good and the evil. When the King of Tyre (Ezekiel 28) goes down to Sheol, many people meet him there. When the prophet Samuel is resting in Sheol after his death, King Saul consults the witch of Endor, a medium who contacts Samuel. The witch doesn't resurrect him, but she makes contact with Samuel, and he says, "Why have you disturbed me?" Samuel seems to be conscious after death.

When the Jews translated the Old Testament into Greek in Alexandria in Egypt a couple of centuries before Jesus, the word *Sheol* was translated *Hades*. I have studied the Septuagint (the Greek version of the Old Testament), and I believe on every occasion, or nearly every occasion, the word *Sheol* is translated *Hades*.

You can also find the concept of Hades in New Testament passages such as Luke 10:13-15, where Jesus says that if you do not repent, you will go down to Hades. I do not think Jesus is saying that you will go to hell—at least not immediately upon your death. Rather, I think he is saying you're going to go down to Hades, the place of the dead, and there will be no opportunity for repentance there. Heaven will not be an option for you, but the idea of going down to Hades reaffirms the teaching of the tripartite universe.

Another familiar passage is found in Matthew 16:18, when Jesus is speaking of the church and he says, "the gates of Hades will not overcome it." Unfortunately, some versions have mistranslated this as "the gates of hell," but that is not what the original language says. In the original language, Matthew 16:18 says, in effect, "The gates of *Hades* will not stand against the kingdom of God." In other words, even if a follower of God died before the time of Jesus, they would not be permanently blocked from redemption through Christ. This also ties in with the ancient doctrine of Jesus going to Hades himself to deliver some kind of proclamation.

As we have established, *Sheol* regularly translates

as *Hades*. Hades is the unseen world, and most scholars believe it comes from the word "to see," or more precisely, "not seen." In the Greek, it is "the unseen place." We do not see Hades, but that does not mean it does not exist. We have all heard skeptics say, "I do not believe in heaven because I do not see it." But let us not be skeptical ourselves when it comes to Hades.

In ancient Greek and Roman mythology, Hades was the underworld, and it was also the name of the god of the underworld. When I mention mythology, that may be somewhat disturbing to some readers, but mythology often contains a grain of truth. And sometimes it contains more than a grain of truth! The Bible writers borrowed the term *Hades* from the Greek language. Of course, the Christian view of Hades is not the same as the Greek view, because in the Greek view, unless you were a god, or especially favored by the gods, you would forever stay in Hades after you died. It was your only choice. Mythology did not share the Christian idea of the resurrection or heaven, so Christianity radically transformed the meaning of the word.

Gehenna

Another word we need to study is *Gehenna*, properly translated as *hell*. The valley of Ben Hinnom, a location mentioned in the Old Testament, is in Jerusalem and is one of the several valleys that intersect the region. It is possible that this valley was a place where fires were kept burning—a kind of perennial trash dump, a place where uncleanness and filth were thrown; a place where corpses, particularly the corpses of the poor, were placed and consumed by worms. It is mentioned in Isaiah 66:24, the last verse of the Prophet Isaiah:

> And they will go out and look upon the dead bodies of those who rebelled against me; their worm will not die, nor will their fire be quenched, and they will be loathsome to all mankind.

This scripture is familiar because Jesus quotes and alludes to it in Matthew 5 and Mark 9 as he talks about the fire of hell. This word he uses for hell, *Gehenna*, relates to the burning and the consumption by worms which, properly speaking, applies to the corpses of those who had rebelled against God. So the word *Gehenna* comes from the idea of the valley of Ben Hinnom.[1] The graphic image portrayed by this word was a familiar image to anyone in Jerusalem, and probably to anyone who came to visit Jerusalem for the various feasts and festivals. Residents and visitors would have been aware of this garbage dump, but there is one more hideous, ignominious activity that took place in the valley of Ben Hinnom: Molech worship.

Molech was one of the popular gods of the Old Testament, and unfortunately, even the Israelites followed him at times. When the Israelites stopped worshiping the Lord God, they also worshiped Baal, Asherah, Molech and many other foreign gods that we read about in the pages of the Old Testament.

Molech was a god who required a terrible sacrifice: your firstborn child. The statue would be heated, a firstborn infant placed in its arms, and the baby would be incinerated.

Molech's followers believed that if you gave up your firstborn child to the god, you would be blessed in terms of fertility (crops, livestock, childbearing, and so forth). Of course, this was a detestable practice to the Lord, but the Israelites sometimes performed this ritual in the valley of Ben Hinnom.

All of this is significant because it helps us understand that the words *Gehenna* and *hell* have a world of history and meaning behind them. These words conjure up vivid images to the thoughtful reader of the Old Testament.

However, some of the early English translations of the Bible made serious errors when translating the words *Gehenna, Hades* and *Sheol.* As an example, let's take the King James Version, which is probably more familiar than its predecessor, the Tyndale version of the mid-1500s. In the King James Version, which was finished in 1611, you will not find the words *Sheol, Hades* or *Gehenna.* In the New Testament and Old Testament, you find only the word hell. In other words, the translators indiscriminately used the word hell for all three words. Now that is quite a mistake, because while Sheol and Hades are the same place, *Gehenna* is not. Sheol and Hades refer to a place of waiting, a temporary place of the dead, but *Gehenna* has to do with the final punishment of the ungodly dead.

We also have the rare word *Tartarus* in 2 Peter 2, which technically is the place where the rebellious angels are kept, but even *Tartarus* is translated as *hell* in the King James. This has led to a number of misconceptions.

The KJV mistranslation is unfortunate because the

original meaning of the words *Sheol* and *Hades* did not necessarily include punishment, and the word *hell* today means something a bit different than what it meant in Anglo-Saxon English, six hundred years or so before King James. The Old English word *helan* meant "to cover over, in the sense of something buried, as in the grave."[2] But by the time of the King James, *hell* had a different connotation, and today that connotation has continued to evolve and change.

Some people think that rebellious humans are kept in *Tartarus* too, and some have suggested that *Tartarus* is the bad part of *Hades*.

The word *Gehenna* is found in a number of places in the New Testament. Jesus said it would be better to enter heaven with one eye, rather than to go to *Gehenna* with both eyes. We find similar references in Matthew 5:22,29,30; Matthew 18:9; and Matthew 23:15,33. The word *Gehenna* appears several times in Mark, and once in Luke. In Matthew 10:28, Jesus says, "Do not fear those who kill the body but cannot kill the soul, but rather fear him who has the power to destroy both soul and body in hell [*Gehenna*]." Based on this and other scriptures, we can conclude that *Sheol* or *Hades* is the intermediate place, but *Gehenna* is the final place of punishment for the wicked.

Paradise

Another key term is *paradise*, as we already saw in Luke 23:43: "Today you will be with me in paradise." We find it also in 2 Corinthians 12:4, where Paul says he was caught up to the third heaven. Then we see it a last time in

Revelation. These are the only three occasions in the New Testament where the word *paradise* is used in this sense.

It seems that paradise means different things, depending on the context. Words do not always have to mean the same thing in every passage—for that reason, we look at many passages, to understand the nuances and multiple meanings of words. For example, Revelation 2:7 says that the person who overcomes will have a chance once again to eat from the tree of life in the paradise of God. In 2 Corinthians and Luke, paradise refers to the intermediate place of the dead, whereas in Revelation, it means something different.

The word translated *paradise* in the Old Testament is translated *paradeisos* in the Greek. As we have mentioned, the Jews translated the Old Testament into the Greek language, and this version of the Bible is called the Septuagint. In the first century (and even before that!), there was a huge Greek-speaking Jewish community in Alexandria, Egypt and throughout the Mediterranean world. So it became necessary to translate the Scriptures into the Greek language. The word *paradeisos*, or paradise, is used in Genesis 1 and 2 to indicate the Garden of Eden. (*Gan* is "garden" in Hebrew; *hagan* is "the garden," especially the Garden of Eden.) It is found again in Ecclesiastes 2, where Solomon said he constructed gardens, and it is found many other times in the Old Testament.

But it can mean other things as well. According to the Oxford English Dictionary, paradise can mean "the garden of Eden"; it can also mean "heaven, the abode of God and his angels and the final abode of the righteous." I do not accept that definition, but I am just listing the meanings this dictionary gives. However, I agree with the third definition: "an intermediate place or state where the departed souls of the righteous await resurrection and the last judgment."[3]

Scholars and theologians agree that many people in ancient times understood paradise to be an intermediate state for the dead, not a final resting place. Paradise is a real place, and we know that because Paul went there.

Let's consider 2 Corinthians 12:1-4 in the New American Standard version:

> Boasting is necessary, though it is not profitable; but I will go on to visions and revelations of the Lord. I know a man in Christ who fourteen years ago—whether in the body I do not know, or out of the body I do not know, God knows—such a man was caught up to the third heaven. And I know how such a man—whether in the body or apart from the body I do not know, God knows—was caught up into Paradise and heard inexpressible words, which a man is not permitted to speak.

As we have said, this is one of three passages in the New Testament where the word *paradise* is used. This passage begs the question: Is Paul describing one place or two? He mentions the third heaven, and then he mentions paradise. Is he mentioning one place by two names, or two separate places, or one place within another place? It's hard to answer those questions based on the Greek, and as we said before, words do not always have to be used the same way in the original Hebrew and Greek.

In this case, we just can't give a definite answer, based on this passage. We just don't know if Paul is using *paradise* to refer to the underworld, or if he is using the word as a synonym for heaven.

It may be that paradise, along with other realities, occupies the space known as the third heaven. I am not dogmatic on this definition, but I have always thought of the third heaven as simply heaven itself. The first heaven would be where the birds fly in the sky, the second heaven is where the stars are, and the third heaven is where God resides. However, the ancient Jews postulated three, seven, or even more heavens, so we don't have enough information in this passage to draw a definitive conclusion.

Second Enoch, a pseudepigraphal book (a book with false authorship), gives us a clue that may be helpful. In 2 Enoch 8-10, the third heaven contains both paradise and hell,[4] so it seems that some ancients conceived of the third heaven as Hades itself. We find a range of ideas in ancient literature, but normally we do not find *paradise* as a synonym for *heaven*.

So the New Testament writers and early Christians considered paradise to be the antechamber, or waiting room, to heaven. As we already read in 2 Peter 2:9, the wicked angels were being held in Tartarus, which is a part of Hades, being punished there before the Day of Judgment. In 2 Peter 2:4-9 we read:

> For if God did not spare angels when they sinned, but sent them to hell, putting them into gloomy dungeons to be held for judgment;

if he did not spare the ancient world when he brought the flood on its ungodly people, but protected Noah, a preacher of righteousness, and seven others; if he condemned the cities of Sodom and Gomorrah by burning them to ashes, and made them an example of what is going to happen to the ungodly; and if he rescued Lot, a righteous man, who was distressed by the filthy lives of lawless men (for that righteous man, living among them day after day, was tormented in his righteous soul by the lawless deeds he saw and heard)— if this is so, then the Lord knows how to rescue godly men from trials and to hold the unrighteous for the day of judgment, while continuing their punishment.

Notice the passage says that God did not spare the wicked angels, but cast them into hell. Unfortunately, most versions say hell, but the Greek text uses the word *Tartarus*, which is not the same thing as hell. Even in the English version, we see that he cast the rebellious angels into hell and committed them to pits of darkness reserved for judgment, which indicates they have not been finally judged yet. Consider verse 9 again: "the Lord knows how to rescue the righteous from trials and keep the godly for the day of judgment." It sounds like the ungodly dead are punished and they cannot escape from that situation, but this is before the day of judgment. In other words, punishment begins even before the punishment day.

The familiar story of the Rich Man and Lazarus was already circulating in at least seven different forms in the first century; it is likely that Jesus tweaked the parable in order to make a point about caring for the needy. Although the passage was probably not intended to give us direct insight into the afterlife, we will proceed in this book with the popular understanding of the passage as describing one's actual post-mortem state.

In Luke 16, the rich man is in Hades, but he is already being punished. Hades is an intermediate place, but it does not mean that the man is just checking into a hotel and relaxing before his sentence is read. The Bible teaches that your fate is sealed at death, and that may be why we find the rich man in Hades already in pain; paradise, however—the part of Hades reserved for the righteous—is a place of reward. But not everyone will go to paradise—not even all the righteous people. If we are alive in the last generation to live on earth, we will be taken directly up to heaven and skip paradise. That truth is revealed in 1 Thessalonians 4:13-18, but again, it does not apply to most Christians—it only applies to those living in the final generation. Chances are that we, and other generations that follow us, will spend some time in paradise before we go to heaven, and like Lazarus, we too will be comforted.

In summary, we have established that the dead, the righteous and unrighteous alike, are all awaiting their final judgment on the Judgment Day. They are waiting in the intermediate place known as Hades, and in some sense they have already begun to receive their punishment or reward. Although the righteous are waiting in the pleasant part of Hades called paradise, no one has gone to heaven yet.

We have also established the existence of *four* places rather than *two*. After death, rather than going immediately to heaven or hell, you go to Hades, which contains two distinct parts—a bad place and a good place. The good place is called paradise and the bad place might be called Tartarus. But whatever its name, it is a place of darkness, a place of punishment, and you don't want to go there! Then we go to heaven or hell *after* the resurrection (that is, the Second Coming, our resurrection and the Judgment Day—we'll explore this idea further in the next chapter). Heaven and hell are the final destinations for which we all are headed.

The End of the World

At the end of time, Jesus will come back. He will usher in the resurrection and the Judgment Day, and we will be sent to our final destination.

Let's take a look at a familiar passage, Acts 2, but focus on the least familiar part: the middle portion. Beginning in Acts 2:23 (New King James Version), we read Peter's words:

Him, being delivered by the determined purpose and foreknowledge of God, you have taken by lawless hands, have crucified, and put to death; whom God raised up, having loosed the pains of death, because it was not possible that He [Christ] should be held by it. For David says concerning Him:

"I foresaw the LORD always before my face,
For He is at my right hand, that I may not be shaken.
Therefore my heart rejoiced, and my tongue was glad;
Moreover my flesh also will rest in hope.
For You will not leave my soul in Hades,

> Nor will You allow Your Holy One to see corruption.
> You have made known to me the ways of life;
> You will make me full of joy in Your presence."

Here the NKJV says that God would not leave Jesus' soul in Hades. Continuing in verses 29-31, we read:

> "Men and brethren, let me speak freely to you of the patriarch David, that he is both dead and buried, and his tomb is with us to this day. Therefore, being a prophet, and knowing that God had sworn an oath to him that of the fruit of his body, according to the flesh, He would raise up the Christ to sit on his throne, he, foreseeing this, spoke concerning the resurrection of the Christ, that His soul was not left in Hades, nor did His flesh see corruption."

What is Peter doing here? He is quoting from Psalm 16, a passage about a descendant of David, the royal king, and the Messiah not being left in Hades. He goes on in verse 32:

> "This Jesus God has raised up, of which we are all witnesses. Therefore being exalted to the right hand of God, and having received from the Father the promise of the Holy Spirit, He poured out this which you now see and hear.
> For David did not ascend into the heavens, but he says himself:
>> "The LORD said to my Lord,
>> 'Sit at My right hand,
>> Till I make Your enemies Your footstool.'"

This ends with a quotation of the Messianic Psalm, Psalm 110, but notice what Peter says right before that—that David did not ascend to heaven.

It is simply not true that if you are right with the Lord you go straight to heaven—both the Old and New Testaments agree on this point. David was a righteous man and a man after God's own heart, yet he did not go to heaven. We also read that the Messiah would go to Hades, but he would not be left there, and he would experience no corruption.

Jesus visited Hades, but he was not left there, because his was a temporary weekend visit. Some preachers mistakenly say that Jesus went to hell, particularly if they are using the King James Version. They say Jesus went to hell but he did not stay there, but it makes no sense to say that Jesus would go to hell, which is the final place of punishment.

If the doctrine I am expounding here is correct, then nobody has gone to hell yet. This understanding is consistent with other passages. In John 3:13, we read, "No one has ascended to heaven but He who came down from heaven, *that is*, the Son of Man, who is in heaven" (NKJV). In this passage, which depicts Jesus' dialogue with Nicodemus, we read that no one has ascended to heaven, and the only one who has ever been in heaven is the one who came out of heaven, the Son of Man. (The Son of Man is one of the terms for the Christ.) So no one is in heaven now (except Jesus) and no one will enter heaven until after the Judgment Day.

In 1 Peter 3:22, we read that after Jesus' resurrection, he went to heaven with angels, authorities and powers in submission to him. Interestingly, if there were people in heaven, why doesn't it say angels, authorities, powers, *and people* in submission to him? There is no mention of people because there are no people in heaven! Jesus must return first, so the Second Coming precedes our going to heaven.

Now take a look at John 14:1-3 (NKJV):

> Let not your heart be troubled; you believe in God, believe also in Me. In My Father's house are many mansions; if *it were* not *so*, I would have told you. I go to prepare a place for you. And if I go and prepare a place for you, I will come again and receive you to Myself; that where I am, *there* you may be also.

What an encouraging passage this is! Jesus reminds people that in his Father's house, there are many rooms, or dwelling places, or mansions, depending on what version of the Bible you read. He says, "I am preparing a place for you," but when do we get to enjoy those heavenly dwelling places? Jesus says that he will go to prepare a place for us and then he will come back and take us to be with him. We will only go to our heavenly dwelling places when the Lord has come back for us. But Jesus does not come back to get us every time someone dies. He will come back during what is commonly called the Second Coming, the return of Christ. (We get the term "Second Coming" from Hebrews 9:26-28.)

So Jesus is going to come back and take us to be with him in heaven at the Second Coming, but I think all Christians agree that the Second Coming has not yet happened. And so we can see that no one has been taken to heaven yet.

1 Peter 5:4 teaches this same truth: "And when the Chief Shepherd appears, you will receive the crown of glory that will never fade away." This passage is talking about elders, urging them to be examples to the flock, and promising that when the Chief Shepherd appears, they will receive a crown of glory that will never fade away. When do we receive the crown of glory? When the Shepherd appears. The Chief Shepherd is Jesus Christ, and when he comes again, *then* we will receive the crown of glory, but not before. Again we see that no one is in heaven yet—and no one is in hell yet, either.

John 5:28-29 says,

Do not marvel at this; for the hour is coming in which all who are in the graves will hear His voice and come forth—those who have done good, to the resurrection of life, and those who have done evil, to the resurrection of condemnation.

What is Christ saying here? A time is coming when all who are in the tombs will hear his voice. So when Jesus returns, he will give the command just as he did with Lazarus (although technically, that was more of a resuscitation than a resurrection, because Lazarus didn't have a resurrected body and would one day die again!). When Jesus gives the command, all will come out of their graves.

He is not talking about two resurrections, but one. This is sometimes called the general resurrection. After this, some will be judged and sent to hell. Here we are talking about eternal judgment. Others will enjoy life that is eternal

life. But this happens immediately after the Second Coming—
it has not yet happened.

The Old Testament word *shamayim*, which we translate "heaven," is used in all three senses. I mentioned before the levels of heaven: where the birds fly, where the stars
are, and where the Lord is. In the New Testament, the Greek
word *ouranos* also encompasses all three levels of meaning.
The name of the planet Uranus comes from this word, and it
simply means heaven. So the word heaven can have various
senses, but if we're careful Bible students, we won't jump to
formulate doctrines based on incomplete information.

As for the nature of heaven, many preachers get that
part right. In this book we will focus more on explaining
what paradise is, because the concept of the intermediate
state is so universally misunderstood.

As we already discovered, the biblical teaching was
gradually changed as the church became Catholic. The Protestants overreacted and omitted the intermediate state, and
that basically became our common modern doctrine—that we
die and we don't go to purgatory, but we don't go to the intermediate state of Hades either. We go straight to heaven.

But the original doctrine actually makes a lot
more sense, and it enables us to harmonize the Scriptures
logically. What do I mean by this? In Revelation, for example,
we read that Hades and death will be thrown into the lake
of fire. If Hades is hell and hell is the lake of fire, how can
hell be thrown into itself? But if Hades and hell are different
places, we have no difficulty. Once again, *I can't emphasize
enough how much damage was done to people's understanding of*

the Scriptures when translators decided to render Hades as hell. They simply are not the same thing; they're totally different places.

This understanding also makes more sense of the Old Testament. *Sheol* is a place where there is some sort of consciousness after death, but it's a dark, shadowy existence and it's not the final resting place. This understanding of Scripture explains why the New Testament affirms that no one is in heaven.

This interpretation also allows for the spiritual body that Paul mentioned in 1 Corinthians 15. In 1 Corinthians 15, Paul explains that we will be resurrected, but we will still have a body. It will be transformed, but only with the resurrection body can we go to heaven. Our bodies are not resurrected when we're in Sheol or Hades. And this makes more sense logically. How can you go to heaven before the resurrection? The resurrection would have to come first.

If you accept this understanding of the afterlife, you can now read all the passages about the intermediate state of the dead without having to gloss over them, and you don't have to speed up and read past the middle of Acts 2. This interpretation makes sense of all scriptures.

In Summary

Chances are, many of you reading this book have never been exposed to the biblical doctrine of Hades, and you may be in a bit of shock, because believing this doctrine requires you to let go of popular misconceptions and to accept the existence of four places rather than two.

When I first heard this notion in 1980, I dismissed it. It seemed cumbersome—not elegant enough. A few years later, I read about it in Edward Fudge's *The Fire That Consumes*.[5] But I still wasn't willing to come on board, at least not for another ten or fifteen years. Then I changed my mind. It wasn't because I was particularly attracted to the doctrine—after all, it seemed harder to understand, and I had heard the traditional view taught for so many years. But over time, I came to embrace this doctrine because of the scriptural evidence, and the first time I taught it was in a book that I published in 1996. Up to that point, I had taught thousands of people the traditional view—and here I was, changing my mind! I believe it is never too late to give up our prejudices. A noble student of the Bible will study, reconsider, examine the scriptural and historical evidence, and ultimately embrace the truth whenever we find it—even if the truth is different from what we've always believed.

Chapter 2

What the Early
Christians Believed

In this chapter, we will move from a study of what the Scriptures teach to a study of what early Christian leaders actually taught. We will examine their own words and take a look at what they wrote on this important subject.

Let's clarify some key terms before we delve into the material. *Patristic study* is a study of the church fathers and their writings. "Pater" means *father* in both Latin and Greek, so patristics is the study of the things left behind by the church fathers, particularly in the first few hundred years of the church.

Since the church began around the year AD 30, this would take us up to the 300s. The apostolic era is the era during which the apostles were still alive. After the last apostle died, we move into what is called the sub-apostolic era. "Sub" is from the Latin word meaning "near" or "under," so the sub-apostolic era is full of writings by men who were not far removed from the apostles, in time and in influence. Since they were so closely influenced by the apostles, their teachings give us a good sense of what the early leaders thought and taught. Their writings shed light on our subject, and we'll be looking at a number of quotations from early Christians in the 100s and 200s, and even a few in the 300s.

All of these writings are ante-Nicene, meaning that they were written before an important event in church history called the Council of Nicaea. The Council of Nicaea, over which Constantine the pagan emperor presided in the year AD 325, was an assembly called to settle some disputes about the nature of Christ, and that council was a major turning point in church history. It is beyond the scope of this book to explain its significance, but with the Council of Nicaea, for all intents and purposes, the church-state was born.

It is important to understand that the writings before AD 325 reflect a different situation than the one that followed the Council of Nicaea. Before the Council, the church was a minority and often faced intense persecution.

My Story

I became interested in the patristic writings when I was earning my Masters in Theological Studies at Harvard Divinity School. I had always known that some writings had been left behind from the early Christian leaders, and I knew that some of my friends had read them, but until then, I hadn't been particularly interested. But as I began to read, I became fascinated with the subject.

I can remember spending many warm days sitting outside reading the words of Clement or Ignatius or the various early church fathers—men who came to mean a great deal to me. Eventually, I collected all of their writings. They are compiled in several dozen volumes, beginning with the early patristics, in the late first century, all the way up to the post-Nicene writings of the 300s through the 700s. And if you walk from one end to the other of that mini-library, left to right, you can literally see doctrine evolving as you go forward in time, growing more complex over time. And if you go backwards, the doctrines become less complicated, less convoluted. But as you go backwards in time, you also see faith burning brightly. Of course I'm not saying that there was no faith after Nicaea, but before Nicaea, Christians lived in a very different environment, a much more challenging one in which their faith was constantly tested and threatened. Studying church history helps us to understand the evolution of wrong teaching, and we certainly have much to learn from that. But it also shows us the roots of various ideas—concepts that began simply, almost like embryos, but developed later on—ideas like the doctrine of the Trinity, or predestination.

How to Read the Patristic Writings

David Berçot is a scholar who has done much to bring the writings of the church fathers to the attention of the English-speaking world. Berçot and I became acquainted in 1995, and we have become friends over the years. I have listened to nearly all of his lessons (there are over 100) and read all of his books.

One of his most useful and interesting books is *A Dictionary of Early Christian Beliefs*, a compilation of quotations from the church fathers, arranged topically.[1] But

Berçot warns that we need to use the patristic writings with care, just as we use the Bible. If we're not careful, we can misuse them just as we misuse scriptures.

Berçot says that the most common mistake we could make would be to employ the patristic writings (and especially Berçot's dictionary) as a database for proof-texts. It would be tempting to sift through it, noting quotations that bolster our personal beliefs and disregarding those that don't fit. That approach is always wrong when it's applied to the Bible, and it's wrong with the patristics, too. By selectively using quotations, we make it appear that the early Christians believed exactly as we do, which is not always the case. In short, instead of learning from those who were closest to the apostles in both time and spirit, we simply use their writings for our own designs.

Another common mistake is to read the early Christian writings too meticulously, as though the writers were making dogmatic theological pronouncements every time they wrote. Although theology was important to the early church, it took a backseat to living the Christian life. Generally, the ante-Nicene Christian writers were not attempting to define precise points of doctrine for the rest of the church. Most of their theological discussions came up in the context of either explaining to outsiders what Christians believed or refuting error—contrasting the tenets of particular heretics with what the general body of Christians believed. They were not necessarily trying to convince other orthodox Christians what to believe.

And you'll notice from some of the quotations in this

series that some of the ancient writers didn't agree with one another. They agreed broadly on the general truths, but not always on every little specific.

Berçot warns that we must also be careful not to read technical or post-Nicene meanings into theological terms used by pre-Nicene Christians. Very rarely did orthodoxy (itself a fifth-century term) turn on the issue of using this word instead of that word. The early Christians understood orthodoxy in terms of concepts, not meticulously theological definitions. Berçot quotes Clement of Alexandria, a writer in the 200s: "Those who are particular about words and devote their time to them miss the point of the whole picture."[6] This is not to say that we don't need to study. Actually, Clement of Alexandria was an enormously diligent student; the point is not to miss the big picture.

Like Berçot, I have a high regard for the patristics. I enjoy reading the first fathers, but I think we need to keep in mind these three caveats. I don't believe the patristics are inspired writings, but they do point to the inspired text, and they can help us in our search for answers.

What the Early Church Fathers Said About the Afterlife

Having laid out the ground rules for reading the patristics, I would like to begin by looking at what the early church said about Hades and paradise.

Let's begin with Justin Martyr. Justin was a philosopher-turned-Christian who was killed for his faith. He wrote this passage around the year AD 160. Keep in mind, he was writing just four or five generations after the resurrection.

He wrote, "The souls of the pious remain in a better place, while those of the unjust and wicked are in a worse, waiting for the time of judgment."[3] Here we have a man living in the sub-apostolic era, saying that the souls of the godly and ungodly are in different places, all awaiting judgment. He doesn't say anything about them already being in heaven or having gone through the judgment. They are *waiting* for the time of judgment. Of course, this passage, in itself, has no authority. But because it's congruent with what the Scriptures say, it does have great value in illustrating what the early Christians believed for quite a long time, and it is in agreement with what we read in John 5 and John 14.

If we move ahead almost forty years, we come to the time of Tertullian. Tertullian was a north African lawyer, one of the most colorful patristic writers I have read. He wrote,

> And if we speak of Paradise, the place of heavenly bliss appointed to receive the spirits of the saints, severed from the knowledge of this world by that fiery zone as by a sort of enclosure...[4]

Now that's a bit of an unusual quotation, but it describes paradise not as the place our bodies go, but a place to receive the spirit of the saints. Also notice he says that it's a place of divine bliss. It's not a place where people are unconscious; there's great happiness there. And yet as he mentions the departed saints (meaning *any* Christian who has died), they are cut off from the knowledge of this world. In other words, in his opinion, they didn't know what was happening on the earth. So we have paradise here, but no mention of heaven.

Let's now move ahead another fifty years or so to AD 250, the time of Cyprian, another early church father. Now I have to warn you that we're coming into the mid-third century, and by this time, a number of wrong doctrines are blossoming. For example, Cyprian pushed the teaching of clergy-laity—the idea that a Christian leader is a clergyman, or a priest. Of course, in the New Testament era, such thinking would have been rejected, since according to 1 Peter 2:9, we're all priests. In a sense, Jesus is our high priest (according to Hebrews 3:1, 4:14, 9:11), and he is the only one who can serve as an intercessor between Christians and God. But on some levels, all Christians serve as priests, because we bring God to the world and we bring the world to God. However, we're not priests for one another.

I mention this so you will realize that, even in AD 250, when a number of wrong doctrines were beginning to blossom, the teaching about paradise was still consistent with what we read in the New Testament. Cyprian wrote,

> We regard Paradise as our country—we already begin to consider the patriarchs as our parents: why do we not hasten and run, that we may behold our country, that we may greet our parents? There a great number of our dear ones is awaiting us, and a dense crowd of parents, brothers, children, is longing for us, already assured of their own safety, and still solicitous for our salvation.[5]

Here we have the idea of paradise, and it seems to fit well with Hebrews 11, which says that Christians are not looking for an earthly city or a terrestrial home, but for something beyond. Paradise is our country, so why don't we hurry to see our country and greet our loved ones awaiting us there? The idea is that they've crossed on ahead; they're waiting for us there. Again, no mention is made of heaven. Paradise is simply where the departed are.

There's no doubt about the position of the early church on this subject, and I could have supplied many more passages from the patristics to bolster this point. But I believe these examples will suffice.

The Gnostic Position

Often you can learn a lot about a topic by studying not just the positive position, but the opposing position as well. Gnosticism was a serious threat to the church in the first century, and even more of a threat in the second century. The letters of 1 and 2 John were written largely to protect the church from Gnostic errors, and we also see the proto-Gnostic ideas refuted in Colossians, 1 Timothy, and 1 Corinthians. Gnostics did not believe in the intermediate state of the dead, but before we look at their views on heaven, let's quickly summarize their teachings.

Gnosticism comes from the Greek word *gnosis*, meaning "knowledge." Gnostics did not believe that God had come in the flesh, nor did they believe in the resurrection. They taught that the world had been created by an inferior God, and pointed to disease, suffering, pain and death as evidence of that creator's inferiority. The Gnostics were so "spiritual" that they believed the flesh was evil and should not be resurrected. The flesh was just a trap—it kept your corpse of a body here on earth, so by all means, you should want to be free from your body. And that's why they denied the resurrection. Upon death, your superfluous body is discarded and your soul proceeds immediately to heaven.

With that in mind, let us look once again at the words of Justin Martyr (writing in about AD 160):

> For if you have fallen in with some who are called Christians, [he's referring here to Gnostics] but who do not admit this [truth], and venture to blaspheme the God of Abraham, and the God of Isaac, and the God of Jacob; who say there is no resurrection of the dead and that their souls, when they die, are taken to heaven; do not imagine that they are Christians."

We see that some second-century Christians had fallen in with the Gnostics; the Gnostics deny the intermediate state; and Justin Martyr says, "do not imagine that they are Christians"! Now I hope this quotation won't be misused. I'm not suggesting that if your preacher espouses the traditional view (that when you die you go straight to heaven), he's a non-Christian. I would rather say that many modern preachers are confused about paradise and heaven and the general order of things, but they're not denying the resurrection; they're not saying the creator God is an evil God created by another being ultimately created by the true God! And they're not saying that you're saved by knowledge. Gnostics were not Christians for *many* reasons, not just their mistaken beliefs about the afterlife.

Let's look at the view of another church father,

Irenaeus. Irenaeus, a church leader in Lyon, France, wrote around AD 180. He wrote:

> But these men are in all points inconsistent with themselves, when they decide that all souls do not enter into the intermediate place, but those of the righteous only.[7]

Apparently, there was a variety of Gnosticism that said the intermediate place is only for the righteous.

Gnostics believed in increasing levels of sophistication and enlightenment, and so some thought that after the righteous died, they went to an intermediate place to be gradually perfected, promoted and upgraded. But they also said that the wicked would not go to the intermediate place. But Scripture teaches that everybody goes there, and that Sheol/Hades is the fate of all. Gnostics also taught that Christ descended into Hades so that we would not need to go there. So you see that even the Gnostics acknowledged that Jesus went into Hades, or the underworld. They were partly right and partly wrong on that point, but their overall interpretation was rejected by the church.

Irenaeus also said the following, in reference to Luke 6:40:

> "No disciple is above the Master, but everyone that is perfect shall be as his Master," as our Master, therefore, did not at once depart, taking flight [to heaven], but awaited the time of His resurrection prescribed by the Father, which had been also shown forth through

Jonas, and rising again after three days was taken up [to heaven];
so ought we also to await the time of our resurrection, prescribed
by God.[8]

Irenaeus said that Jesus didn't go straight to heaven
when he died. He had to wait until his resurrection, and we
are in the same position. No disciple is above his master,
and in this case, quite literally, we're not going to be above
Jesus. We're not going to rise above the underworld and go
straight to heaven before our resurrection. Instead, there is
a sequence to everything.

Now let me share some writings from Hippolytus, a
patristic writer who wrote at the very close of the second
century, around AD 195:

But now we must speak of Hades, in which the souls both of the
righteous and the unrighteous are detained. Hades is a place in
the created system, rude, a locality beneath the earth, in which the
light of the world does not shine; and as the sun does not shine in
this locality there must necessarily be perpetual darkness there.

We can see the cosmology in this saying:

This locality has been destined to be as it were a guard house
for souls, at which the angels are stationed as guards, distributing
temporary punishments for different characters. And in this locality
there is a certain place set apart by itself, a lake of unquenchable
fire into which we suppose no one has ever yet been cast; for
it is prepared against the day determined by God, in which one

sentence of righteous judgment shall be justly applied to all. But
the righteous shall obtain the incorruptible and unfading kingdom,
who indeed are at present detained in Hades, but not in the same
place with the unrighteous."[9]

He describes Hades as having two parts: one part for
the righteous and another for the unrighteous. The righteous
are separated from the unrighteous, and the unrighteous are
being punished. But these are simply temporary placements.
Hippolytus also mentions the lake of fire, which he believes
is in Hades. Where it is doesn't really matter. But the salient
point is that Hippolytus doesn't believe anyone has actually
gone into the lake of fire yet. I believe his view represents the
common view of the church, even as late as AD 200.

Hippolytus continues:

"For to this locality there is one descent, at the gate whereof we
believe an archangel is stationed with a host. And when those who
are conducted by the angels appointed unto the souls have passed
through this gate, they do not proceed on one and the same way;
but the righteous being conducted in the light toward the right, and
being hymned by the angels stationed at the place, are brought
to a locality full of light. And there the righteous from the beginning dwell, not ruled by necessity, but enjoying always the con-
templation of the blessings which are in their view, and delighting
themselves with the expectation of others ever new; and deeming
those ever better than these. And that place brings no toils to them.
There is neither fierce heat, nor cold, nor thorn; but the face of the
fathers and the righteous is seen to be always smiling, as they wait

for the rest and eternal revival in heaven that succeeded this location. And we call it by the name *Abraham's bosom*.[10]

So he's described the good part of Hades, and one of
these places is Abraham's bosom. That should be familiar to
you from the story Jesus told in Luke 16.

Now let's look at the other group, the unrighteous.
Hippolytus says that when the righteous go into Hades, they
are ushered off to the right. However,

The unrighteous are dragged toward the left by angels who are
ministers of punishment, and they go of their own accord no
longer, but are dragged by force as prisoners. And the angels
appointed over them send them along, reproaching them and
threatening them with an eye of terror, forcing them down into the
lower parts. And when they are brought there, those appointed to
that service drag them on to the confines of hell. And those who
are so near hear incessantly the agitation, and feel the hot smoke.
And when that vision is so near, as they see the terrible and
excessively glowing spectacle of the fire, they shudder in horror
at the expectation of the future judgment, (as if they were) already
feeling the power of the punishment. And again, where they see
the place of the fathers and the righteous, they are also punished
there. For a deep and vast abyss is set there in the midst so neither
can any of the righteous in sympathy think to pass it, nor do any of
the unrighteous dare to cross it.[11]

Again, this sounds very similar to Luke 16 and the
story of the rich man and Lazarus. In that story told by Jesus, an
impassable chasm separates the two groups. And Hippolytus

says the punishment of the unrighteous has three different facets. One is the simple realization that the righteous are having such a wonderful time while the unrighteous are not. They can only contemplate and regret their choices. Another form of punishment is that they are already suffering from the heat of the nearby lake of fire. (Have you ever been too close to fire and gotten a bit scorched?) The third aspect of their torment is the expectation of their future suffering in the lake of fire. They live with the awful knowledge that on Judgment Day they will be destroyed in the lake of fire.

We'll conclude with one other quotation from Hippolytus:

> Thus far on the subject of Hades, in which all souls are detained until the time which God has determined; and then He will accomplish a resurrection of all, not by transferring souls into other bodies, but by raising the bodies themselves.[12]

Here we have his view of resurrection. Resurrection doesn't mean that you get someone else's body as some transmodification or reincarnation. No, your own body resurrects, but it's transformed. This view was taught consistently by the orthodox church. I could mention many other passages to support this.

For example, let's go even later in time, to the year AD 290, to the writings of a man named Methodius:

> But the rich man in torment, and the poor man who was comforted in the bosom of Abraham, are said, the one to be punished in

Hades, and the other to be comforted in Abraham's bosom, before the appearing of the Savior, and before the end of the world, and therefore, before the resurrection…[13]

According to him, there is punishment and reward before the end of the world, before the second coming, the resurrection and the final judgment.

In the fourth century, Lactantius wrote:

Nor, however let anyone imagine that souls are immediately judged after death. For all are detained in one and a common place of confinement, until the arrival of the time in which the great Judge shall make an investigation of their deserts.[14]

What was Lactantius saying here? He said we're not judged immediately after death. Of course, all of these men believed that once you died your fate was sealed, but this is referring to the Judgment Day itself. Lactantius also said that the good and the bad are detained in a common place of confinement. Hades has different divisions, but everyone is there. And they will not stay there forever, but only until the time when the Judge will send them to their final destinations.

Having read all this, consider this shocking perspective: If you were to somehow be transported back to talk to an apostle or an early Christian (particularly one who lived in the 300s, 200s, 100s or the first century), and you told them that when Christians died they went straight to heaven, you would be taken for a heretic!

The Early Church's Views on Hell and Purgatory

Let's look in greater detail at some of the church fathers' specific teachings about the nature of the afterlife.

• Everlasting Flames

The early Christians tended to interpret the flames of hell (or *Gehenna*) as everlasting. Eternity, in a biblical sense, has more of a notion of quality than quantity. We often think that *eternal* is a synonym for *infinite duration*—that it means the same thing as everlasting. And the word can be used that way. However, normally in the Bible—in both testaments—the word that we translate as *eternal* is not used that way at all. But most of the patristics interpreted the flames in what I would call the traditional sense (the Catholic sense): that those thrown into the flames would be alive forever and ever and ever in torment. And a number of them said that God would continually renew their flesh so that it wouldn't be destroyed or consumed, but they would continue to feel the pain forever and ever.

That's a powerful teaching. I wrote a paper on my understanding of the nature of hell, which was published over two decades ago and is included in this book as an appendix. I certainly don't deny that the judgment is eternal, but I do question our understanding of what eternity means. To summarize my position, I believe hell doesn't last infinitely, but instead destroys the individual after an appropriate length of time. Hell is eternal in its *consequences*, not in its *duration*. We will delve further into the idea of hell in chapter four, and in the appendix.

• The Evolution of Purgatory

Before we close this chapter, let's look at one more idea that the early church gradually came to accept and teach: the concept of purgatory, a place where those who are not quite good enough have their sins burned off. As I studied the patristic writings, I was surprised by what I found. I had thought that the notion of purgatory evolved over time and came into full flower around the year 400 or so, after a few generations of rule by the Catholic Church. But this idea of purgatory actually developed earlier.

I'm going to begin again with Tertullian, who wrote during the third century. I quoted him before because I agreed with him, and I'm quoting him now because I disagree with him. (You see, I'm trying to practice what I preach by quoting people I sometimes disagree with!) Tertullian wrote this:

Therefore as it has acted in each several instance so proportionally does it suffer in Hades being the first to taste judgment the process of that judgment that is postponed to the last great day.[15]

His idea was that the soul suffers proportionately. Perhaps he based his belief on a passage like Luke 12:47. Regardless of where he got this idea, I believe he set the stage for the concept of Hades to morph into the modern Catholic idea of purgatory. Now Hades does not become purgatory in the early 200s. And I even agree with his concept of proportional suffering, but I think he planted a seed that will later germinate into a new doctrine.

Forty years later, Cyprian wrote this:

> It is one thing, tortured by suffering for sins, to be cleansed and
> long purged by fire; another to have purged all sins by suffering. It
> is one thing, in fine, to be in suspense till the sentence of God at
> the day of judgment; another to be at once crowned by the Lord.[16]

So what he is saying here is that you don't go immediately to heaven. There is a period before that, a period of suspense, a period of purgation, and you can see how the later writers would quote people like Cyprian and even Tertullian to say they had justification for the doctrine of purgatory.

Origen, writing in 225, was one of the most intellectual writers of the third century. He envisioned paradise as a classroom, and if you learned your lessons, you could advance and eventually you'd go to heaven. That sounds a little bit more like the Catholic idea than the early church idea.

So this idea of purgatory was rare. It certainly wasn't dominant in the Christian literature in the ante-Nicene period. In the fourth century, this would change, and by the end of that century, by the year 400, purgatory was a common idea.

But why would the early church embrace a notion as bizarre as purgatory? It's not quite as strange as you might think, even though it is unscriptural. Remember that in the early days of Christianity, it was difficult to become a Christian. I don't mean it was hard because church leaders set up obstacles to prevent new members from joining the fold; rather, it was challenging because Christianity was counter-cultural and because, very often, Christians faced persecution.

As church and politics became intertwined, Christianity was legalized and ultimately, in 381, it became the imperial religion of the Roman Empire. In the early 300s, only a minority in the Empire were Christians, probably no more than ten percent. But by the end of the fourth century, floods of new members were pouring in from the world. Once Christianity became the sanctioned religion, you couldn't hold political office if you weren't a Christian. Everyone was getting "converted." By the end of the 300s, nearly everybody in the Roman Empire had been baptized.

Millions of members were coming into the church from the world, and yet they were not repenting. And the priests (they called themselves clergymen at the time) knew that, and had to shepherd congregations that were mostly filled with worldly people. So they began to speculate that after death, there must be some opportunity for purification—that people could become worthy, but they would have to suffer for it. But nothing in the Scriptures supports this. So what passages would proponents of purgatory produce? Typically, they would turn to 1 Corinthians 3. And yet, as we will see, this is not a passage about our lives in purgatory—it's about our work of ministry on this earth. If you go back to the beginning of chapter 3 to find the context, it's talking about church planting and ministry. In 1 Corinthians 3:11-15, Paul says:

> For no one can lay any foundation other than the one already laid, which is Jesus Christ. If any man builds on this foundation using gold, silver, costly stones, wood, hay or straw, his work will be shown for what it is, because the Day will bring it to light. It will be revealed with fire, and the fire will test the quality of each man's work. If what he has built survives, he will receive his reward. If it is burned up, he will suffer loss; he himself will be saved, but only as one escaping through the flames.

Although this passage is talking about the quality of church building and has nothing to do with our personal righteousness, people seized upon the image of someone escaping through the flames as through a burning building, and applied it far beyond the original scope of the illustration itself. Despite that, the church fathers gradually began to believe that, in Hades, some sort of purification might be affected.

In Summary

When we studied what the early Christians taught about Hades and paradise, we saw that their teaching matched what we read in the Bible itself. But the Gnostic position—the heretical position—triumphed in the end. Although Gnosticism was suppressed by the Catholic Church, some stubborn teachings remained, survived the Protestant Reformation in the 1500s, and still influence the way most modern Christians think about the afterlife. And so the Gnostic view—that you go to heaven immediately when you die—is the one embraced and taught by most Protestants and

Catholics to this very day.

We have touched on the origins of the doctrine of purgatory, which became more important in the fifth century, when the churches become worldly. But one concept is unassailable: Hades. The Bible and the patristic writers overwhelmingly agree: There is an intermediate state of the dead.

Although the patristic writers don't speak with any biblical authority, their writings do allow us to draw certain inferences. They illustrate biblical doctrines and help us to reconstruct what doctrinal evolutions may have occurred between the New Testament time and the sub-apostolic era. Patristic evidence illustrates, but it does not prove. A thorough study of the writings of the church fathers shows that, while the early writers do not agree on every detail concerning Hades, there is a remarkable consensus on the fact that the dead do not go straight to heaven or hell. All these ancient writers uphold the intermediate state of the dead. The only exception is the heretics, the Gnostics.

The Bible, along with supporting evidence from the early Christian writings, reveals that Christianity today has virtually abandoned the original biblical teaching on the afterlife.

Chapter 3

Problems and Objections

You probably have some questions and objections to this teaching by now. The purpose of this chapter is to address some of the specific difficulties people have with these concepts.

I have no problem with objections—they mean you are thinking for yourself! As I travel around the world teaching the Bible, I always encourage people to study and debate issues of faith for themselves, just as Paul urged the Thessalonians to test everything. 1 Thessalonians was written in AD 50, when most of the apostles were still alive, yet Paul still warned them, "Do not put out the Spirit's fire; do not treat prophecies with contempt. Test everything. Hold on to the good. Avoid every kind of evil" (1 Thessalonians 5:19-22). If people still needed to filter what they heard, even in "the age of inspiration," surely we should be filtering what we hear today, two thousand years after Christ. As Carl Sagan, the famous atheist said, "Keep your baloney detector on!"

A theory needs to take all the facts into account. At first the idea that we go to heaven indirectly (after passing through Hades) may seem complicated. But I believe it actually makes sense of all the data—all the scriptures, all the teachings of the early church fathers—that we have to process.

Let's now consider thirteen specific objections.

Objection 1: *If we go to Hades first, why isn't it emphasized more in the New Testament?*

If I told you that I was flying to London tomorrow, you wouldn't think I was being dishonest if I neglected to mention that my flight had a layover in New York. Even if I waited there for a number of hours, my final destination would still be London. In the same way, although we will experience a kind of layover in Hades or paradise, that's really not our ultimate destination. And that may also explain why Hades is not emphasized all that much in the New Testament.

You might say, "Well, doesn't Paul say in Philippians 1:23 that he desires to depart and be with the Lord? This makes it sound like he's going to be with the Lord right away." Yes Paul does say that, and there are a couple of ways you could view his statement. First, as I said, the time in paradise is really just a layover. Another perspective would be that the Lord is somehow with us in Hades (or paradise or Sheol). In fact, if you look at Psalm 139, you'll see that his presence is everywhere, so however you cut it, it's certainly true that when we die, we will be with the Lord.

Objection 2: *In the story of the rich man and Lazarus, wasn't Lazarus already in heaven and the rich man already in hell?*

Let's take a closer look at this passage:

> There was a rich man who was dressed in purple and fine linen and lived in luxury every day. At his gate was laid a beggar named Lazarus, covered with sores and longing to eat what fell from the rich man's table. Even the dogs came and licked his sores.
>
> The time came when the beggar died and the angels carried him to Abraham's side. The rich man also died and was buried. In hell, where he was in torment, he looked up and saw Abraham far away, with Lazarus by his side. So he called to him, 'Father Abraham, have pity on me and send Lazarus to dip the tip of his finger in water and cool my tongue, because I am in agony in this fire.'
>
> But Abraham replied, "Son, remember that in your lifetime you received your good things, while Lazarus received bad things, but now he is comforted here and you are in agony. And besides all this, between us and you a great chasm has been fixed, so that those who want to go from here to you cannot, nor can anyone cross over from there to us." (Luke 16:19–26)

There's more to this passage, but this section gives us enough for our purposes. We see the righteous and unrighteous dead being relatively close together, but with a chasm between them. It's difficult to explain what that chasm is if Jesus is depicting heaven and hell, but it's very easy if he is describing Hades. And then we have the phrase "Abraham's bosom" (used in other translations, including the New King James Version), which the early church understood to refer to paradise, or the intermediate place of the dead. There is also mention of the heat, and the man is clearly suffering for his sin.

Keep in mind what we discussed in chapter one: The word *hell* comes from a mistranslation of the word *Hades.* This has led countless people to misunderstand this parable (and other scriptures as well). Although this error is most unfortunate, many modern versions have translated this passage correctly.

I will list here just a few of the accurate translations:

- The New Jerusalem Bible: *"In his torment in Hades he looked up"*
- The New Living Translation: *"The rich man also died and was buried, and his soul went to the place of the dead. There, in torment, he saw Abraham"* (This translation is a bit more descriptive, and it is helpful, although it's a bit more of a paraphrase.)
- The New Revised Standard: *"In Hades, where he was being tormented"*
- The New American Standard: *"In Hades he lifted up his eyes"*
- The Holman Christian Standard: *"And being in torment in Hades"*
- The New King James: *"And being in torments in Hades"*

But the NIV, which is the best-selling English Bible today, unfortunately says "hell," with just a footnote to alert the reader to the fact that the translators chose not to translate the word literally. Maybe they did this out of pressure of tradition—I don't really know—but it is no wonder that so many readers are confused.

So what do we conclude? Readers often presume that Abraham's bosom and the flames of torment were the eternal destinies for Lazarus and the rich man. But the text never says that. The text clearly says that they were in Hades, the intermediate state of the dead. But we've imported the wrong idea from other places, and we have heard it preached so often that it's difficult not to interpret it in the traditional way.

Objection 3: *Isn't Hades the same thing as hell?*

We have already established that *Hades* is not the same thing as hell. Sometimes I hear people swearing or taking mild oaths, and they use the word Hades as a circumlocution for hell. But it's not the same thing because, as I mentioned before, Revelation 20 tells us that Hades will one day be thrown into hell:

> The sea gave up the dead that were in it, and death and Hades gave up the dead that were in them, and each person was judged according to what he had done. Then death and Hades were thrown into the lake of fire. (Revelation 20:13-14)

It talks about the sea and death and Hades giving up their dead. In this passage, death and Hades are probably one way of describing the same thing.

The lake of fire in verse 14 seems to be talking about the fire of hell, doesn't it? But notice that death and Hades are thrown into the fire. So if Hades is hell, how can Hades be thrown into itself? That would make no sense at all.

All this helps us to see that one day, there will be no need for an intermediate place. Everyone will be going to their final destinations. Hades and hell are two different places.

Objection 4: *But didn't Jesus say the thief on the cross would meet him in heaven that day?*

First, Jesus never said he would meet the thief in heaven that day. He said he would meet him in *paradise*. So we have to begin by defining terms and understanding what Jesus meant by the word *paradise*. Normally in the Bible, paradise is talking about the intermediate state of the dead. So the thief was not going to meet Jesus in heaven.

Second, Jesus hadn't yet ascended to heaven at that time. He didn't ascend until weeks later. After he was resurrected from the dead, he also told Mary Magdalene not to hold onto him because he hadn't yet ascended to the Father. By Pentecost (which is about fifty days after Easter Sunday), Peter tells us that Jesus has ascended to heaven.

Objection 5: *What about messages from "the other side"?*

This objection might also sound like this: "I had a friend who received a message from someone who died." Or, "One of the saints appeared and told my grandmother something." Or, "Don't we have evidence from people who have gone to heaven?" That's a very common cluster of questions. There is also the cult of the Virgin Mary and the cult of Saints, who believe that... Many people believe that good people who have died are somehow still in contact with the living.

The problem with all this "evidence" from the other side is that there's just no way to prove it. You can't argue *for* it, and you can't argue *against* it. It's just an experience. It's something someone dreamed or heard or thought they saw. But we should be very leery of accepting such experiences as conclusive evidence. The Bible is the filter through which all these things must be interpreted, and none of the common evidence given for life on the other side holds water.

Objection 6: *But what about 1 Samuel 28, where the witch of Endor raised Samuel from the grave?*

This passage is fascinating, and certainly one of the strangest encounters in the entire Bible. It makes us wonder whether people can communicate with the dead. I don't know whether it's possible, but I do know that it's forbidden. Under the Old Testament, there was a death penalty attached to it, and under the New Testament it's called a sin (Galatians 5:20).

Many people don't know how to interpret 1 Samuel 28, and some people use it as evidence to support various unbiblical ideas. Some say the witch of Endor was trying to bring up Samuel and that somehow Satan was involved; some suggest that God only let her *think* she had brought up Samuel from the dead. This is necromancy, the practice of consulting the dead. It's clear that the witch of Endor was very surprised when she saw Samuel. The text suggests that normally she did fake it, but this experience was authentic.

But think about this: If Samuel had died and gone straight to heaven, then this passage would be a problem. How could the witch call Samuel down to earth from heaven? But if Samuel was in a temporary place of rest—if he was in the part of Hades called paradise—then the passage makes sense.

Personally, I don't want to try to consult the dead! But the fact that Samuel was called up causes no problems with the view I'm defending. It actually supports it because of *where* the Bible says Samuel came from. When the medium saw Samuel, she said, "I see a spirit coming up out of the ground." Samuel was not called down from heaven; he was brought up from wherever he was—and I believe he was in the underworld, Hades.

Objection 7: *But what about Stephen? Doesn't the book of Acts say he went straight to heaven?*

With this objection, people are referring to Acts 7:55-59:

> But Stephen, full of the Holy Spirit, looked up to heaven and saw the glory of God, and Jesus standing at the right hand of God. "Look," he said, "I see heaven open and the Son of Man standing at the right hand of God."
>
> At this they covered their ears and, yelling at the top of their voices, they all rushed at him, dragged him out of the city and began to stone him. Meanwhile, the witnesses laid their clothes at the feet of a young man named Saul.

While they were stoning him, Stephen prayed, "Lord Jesus, receive my spirit."

Read this passage carefully. Does it actually say that Stephen died and went to heaven? It says he gazed intently into heaven and saw the glory of God. God allowed him to have a vision of Jesus in heaven. Many people assume that, if he asked Jesus to receive his spirit, he must have been headed exactly where Jesus was: heaven.

Here are the facts: Stephen saw Jesus in heaven at the right hand of God; he knew that the Bible promises comfort to the righteous after death; he knew that when he died he would be a lot closer to the Lord than he could be on earth; so naturally, Stephen called upon the Lord to receive his spirit. His last words were similar to Jesus' own words when he was dying: "Father, into your hands I commit my spirit."

But technically speaking, this passage never says Stephen died and went to heaven. Of course he wanted to go there, and presumably it would be his ultimate destination, later on. But there is nothing in the text to prove that Stephen went straight to heaven at the time of his death. Jesus could have received Stephen's spirit and taken it to paradise, to begin his reward and await his future in heaven.

Objection 8: *What about David's dead son? Doesn't the passage in 2 Samuel 12 say that David expected to go to heaven to meet his dead son?*

Let's take a look at the passage in question, 2 Samuel 12:22-23:

He answered, "While the child was still alive, I fasted and wept. I thought, 'Who knows? The LORD may be gracious to me and let the child live.' But now that he is dead, why should I fast? Can I bring him back again? I will go to him, but he will not return to me."

Some people think that David was saying he would join the little child in heaven. But that's really a circular argument, isn't it? You have to assume what you're trying to prove in order to prove your argument! You have to begin with the assumption that the child died and went to heaven. But does the Bible say that the child died and went to heaven? Not at all! It simply says, "I will go to him, but he will not return to me."

David expected to rejoin his child one day. That thought is biblical. We can expect to be reunited with our loved ones who have died in the Lord. We will see them again. But this text doesn't say that we will see them in heaven initially.

Objection 9: *Doesn't the Bible say that there's no consciousness between death and resurrection? Don't we all just sleep until we get to heaven? Isn't the soul unconscious?*

It is true that scripture mentions the sleep of death. For example, in John 11 Jesus described Lazarus (who was dead at the time) as sleeping. Jesus was using sleep as a metaphor for death; we see this in other places in the Bible as well. 1 Corinthians 11:30 reads, "That is why many among you are weak and sick, and a number of you have fallen asleep." 1 Corinthians 15:51–54 says,

> Listen, I tell you a mystery: We will not all sleep, but we will all be
> changed—in a flash, in the twinkling of an eye, at the last trumpet.
> For the trumpet will sound, the dead will be raised imperishable,
> and we will be changed. For the perishable must clothe itself with
> the imperishable, and the mortal with immortality. When the perish-
> able has been clothed with the imperishable, and the mortal with
> immortality, then the saying that is written will come true: "Death
> has been swallowed up in victory."

We should be careful about reading too much into
passages like these. After all, the entire passage in 1 Corinthians 15 could be taken as an extended metaphor. And so
the question is this: Is sleep intended as more than a metaphor? Are our souls actually unconscious at death?

We find vivid imagery of the talking, conscious dead
in Isaiah 14:

> On the day the LORD gives you relief from suffering and turmoil
> and cruel bondage, you will take up this taunt against the king of
> Babylon:
>
>> How the oppressor has come to an end!
>> How his fury has ended!...
>> The realm of the dead below is all astir
> to meet you at your coming;
> it rouses the spirits of the departed to greet you—
> all those who were leaders in the world;
> it makes them rise from their thrones—

> all those who were kings over the nations.
> They will all respond, they will say to you,
> "You also have become weak, as we are;
> you have become like us." (Isaiah 14:1–10)

At face value, you've got the dead in *Sheol* (Hades, the grave, the intermediate state), all preparing to meet the king of Babylon. So they are not just "out of it" in some catatonic trance. They're actually meeting him. I would be careful how you interpret this passage, but the natural meaning is certainly not that the souls are sleeping.

In the passage we discussed earlier, 1 Samuel 28, the witch of Endor did appear to have disturbed Samuel, so he could have been dozing in paradise. We don't really know, but he was certainly conscious when he had his discussion with Saul.

Let's revisit the passage in Luke 23 about the thief on the cross. How encouraging would it have been if Jesus had told him something like this: "Look, Mr. Thief, today you will be with me in paradise, but you won't even know it because you will be out cold! You'll be fast asleep." I don't think that's what Jesus was saying. They were both going to the same place, and Jesus said he would see him there–this seems to indicate an event where they would both consciously greet one another after they died.

Some people have also referred to Luke 20:38, which indicates that God is outside of time: "He is not the God of the dead, but of the living, for to him all are alive." People argue something like this: *If all humans exist simultaneously for God, and if God is outside of time, that means the dead must already be in heaven.* My response is this: If you're going to say that the dead are already in heaven simply because God is outside of time, then why don't you also say that they're already in hell?

I have no problem with the conclusion that God may exist outside of time. But does that mean that *people* are totally outside of time as well? Does time cease to exist after we die? Or is it transformed? There is a big difference between the two. The nature of time may change in the time to come, but nowhere does the Bible say that for all humans all times coexist simultaneously. That is only true of God.

I certainly believe that our souls rest in Hades. But to say that we're asleep there, and won't wake up until we arrive in heaven, is wrong.

Objection 10: *What about Enoch and Elijah? Didn't they go straight to heaven?*

The Bible never says these men went straight to heaven. It simply says that the Lord took them. In the Holman Christian Standard Version, Genesis 5:24 reads, "Enoch walked with God; then he was not there because God took him." Elijah was caught up by chariots of fire and taken up into the heavens. That's the way he disappeared, but does that mean he went straight to heaven? The Bible doesn't actually say that.

Irenaeus, one of the church fathers we quoted in chapter two, wrote about this topic, around the year 180. He wrote:

> For in Adam the hands of God had become accustomed to set in
> order, to rule, and to sustain His own workmanship, and to bring
> it and place it where they pleased. Where, then, was the first man
> placed? In paradise certainly...Wherefore also the elders who
> were disciples of the apostles tell us that those who were translat-
> ed were transferred to that place (for paradise has been prepared
> for righteous men, such as have the Spirit; in which place also Paul
> the apostle, when he was caught up, heard words which are un-
> speakable as regards us in our present condition), and that there
> shall they who have been translated remain until the consumma-
> tion [of all things], as a prelude to immortality.[1]

Here those who were "translated" refers to Elijah and Enoch, and Irenaeus says they were transferred to paradise until "the consummation of things." Irenaeus used the concept of paradise as the prelude to immortality, and he also explains Paul's experience as a translation, like Elijah and Enoch's experience. According to Irenaeus, all these men were translated and went to paradise. I don't think anyone would say that Paul actually bypassed the resurrection and the Judgment Day and entered heaven. But like Elijah and Enoch, he did go to the third heaven, or paradise. (And unlike Elijah and Enoch, he came back to earth!)

If your head is spinning, I realize these are not easy things to understand. But we are looking for objections that are irrefutable. I have yet to find evidence that refutes the ancient belief in the intermediate state of the dead. Consider this: Even if Enoch and Elijah did go straight to heaven (and I don't think the Scriptures say that), their stories would not disprove the concept of Hades; they would simply serve as an exception to the experience we can all expect to have when we die. Exceptions to the rule tend to actually prove that the rule is true! Or to look at it another way, you wouldn't assume, just because Elijah performed miracles, that you and I should be able to do them as well. Elijah's miraculous deeds are exceptions, and that is why we call them miracles.

However, I do not believe, in this case, that Enoch and Elijah are exceptions to the normal afterlife experience. Based on the scriptural evidence, Enoch and Elijah did not go straight to heaven. The Bible simply says that the Lord took them, and the assumption should be that he took them to paradise.

Objection 11: *What about the cloud of witnesses in Hebrews 12:1-2? Doesn't the Bible say that those in heaven are up there looking down in the grandstands like spectators watching our race?*

Is that really what Hebrews 12 says? Let's look at the passage a little closer:

> Therefore, since we are surrounded by such a great cloud of witnesses, let us throw off everything that hinders and the sin that so easily entangles, and let us run with perseverance the race marked out for us. Let us fix our eyes on Jesus, the author and perfecter of our faith, who for the joy set before him endured the cross, scorning its shame, and sat down at the right hand of the

throne of God.

You always have to study passages in their context. The "therefore" in verse 1 follows Hebrews 11, which mentions a list of faithful men and women. That group of men and women, that cloud of witnesses in this extended metaphor, are apparently in the stadium watching other Christians run their race. Some people take this passage and–pardon the pun–run with it. They jump to conclusions like this: *Our dead Bible heroes, and even our dead loved ones, are in heaven watching over us. They are emotionally engaged in our struggles, cheering us on.* Some people even go so far as to use this passage as justification for praying to the dead for wisdom and guidance! For this reason, it's important to interpret this passage correctly.

I believe the cheering crowd is being used in a metaphorical sense. To be fair, if you're going to argue from this passage that our heroes in the faith are literally watching us, then you must also say that we are literally running a race! But if you interpret this scripture to mean that life is *like* a race, then I would argue it's as *though* our heroes were watching us. But either way, you can't prove that the righteous dead are watching. What do they know about what is happening in our world, in our life on the earth? Perhaps they know something–perhaps not. This scripture is not enough to draw a firm conclusion. And are these heroes already in heaven? This passage doesn't say that they are.

Another important thing to understand is that the

cloud of witnesses here are not our departed loved ones. They are the men and women of faith in the Old Testament. Maybe our Bible heroes are watching us, maybe not. This passage alone does not give us enough to go on. But think about this: *Even if* the cloud of witnesses is watching us, could they not be doing it from paradise?

Objection 12: *If this theory about the intermediate state of the dead is true, and if the traditional teaching about people going straight to heaven is wrong, what about the scholars? Do the experts support this view?*

Well, that depends. I don't normally defer to the experts. Experts often make mistakes; however, I have consulted various sources in my study of this topic.

Easton's Bible Dictionary actually agrees with the definition of Hades and hell that I am supporting in this book.[2] I found there exactly what I have presented in this book. Easton's definitions line up with the beliefs of the early church fathers, with the New Testament and with *Nave's Topical Dictionary*.[3]

I went to *Vine's Complete Expository Dictionary of Old and New Testament Words* and here's a quote from that source: "They spoke of the region of the departed spirits of the lost." And this source also suggests that paradise and heaven may not be exactly the same thing.[4]

At the end of the day, scholars and their study can enrich and inform us. But scholars can be, and often have been, wrong.

Objection 13: *If this teaching is true, then why is no one teaching it?*

Our final objection may be the most obvious one. Actually, many people do teach this idea. Yes, the vast majority of Christians and Christian teachers have let go of it, but there are still many who do subscribe to it. The Greek Orthodox Church's doctrine includes a concept of Hades. A number of evangelicals teach that the dead do not go to heaven or hell, but to the intermediate state. I have been teaching this idea for a number of years, and when I speak, I often ask the audience how many have heard of this notion of Hades. In any audience of one hundred people or more, a few hands always go up. Although it is true that most people have never been taught this view, that doesn't make it false.

In conclusion, none of these objections hold water, and I have yet to find any that do. In this chapter we have considered thirteen of the most common objections to the idea of Hades. But as we have seen, these questions don't disprove the existence of an intermediate state of the dead, and they certainly do not overthrow the idea. If anything, once you explore these objections, you end up confirming the existence of Hades!

Chapter 4

End Times Theology:
Armageddon, Antichrist, Apocalypse

The Second Coming is a hot topic these days. The end times have become something of a pop culture obsession, spawned in part by the *Left Behind* novel series by authors Tim LaHaye and Jerry B. Jenkins. Some of the ideas introduced in these books are biblically accurate; others are not.

People are always looking for signs, and they love the sensational. But not every idea taught in the popular press, embraced by the Christian world at large, or presented in novels and pop-theology books is correct. (And keep in mind that novels are fictional interpretations, not biblical truth.)

The Battle of Armageddon

Many people believe the Second Coming will take place sometime around the battle of Armageddon, an image of war found in Revelation 16. However, I do not believe the battle of Armageddon refers to a literal battle that mankind is destined to endure. The book of Revelation is replete with symbolism, including some five hundred allusions to the Old

Testament. The word *Armageddon* is derived from the Hebrew word *har-Megiddo*, which means hill or mountain of Megiddo. Megiddo was a place where many battles took place in the Old Testament (the earliest recorded "battle of Armageddon" occurred almost 4400 years ago, and there have been numerous battles in the region since), so readers familiar with Bible history know to associate the name Armageddon with warfare. In other words, Armageddon is a symbolic image of warfare, intended to remind us of the battles waged by men of God there from time immemorial.[1]

The Rapture and the Tribulation

Although I disagree with the popular idea that a literal battle awaits all of mankind before Jesus returns, I do accept the overall concept of the rapture. The general idea of the rapture—that Christians who are alive when Jesus returns will be caught up in the clouds to meet the Lord—is confirmed by 1 Thessalonians 4:13-18:

> Brothers, we do not want you to be ignorant about those who fall asleep, or to grieve like the rest of men, who have no hope. We believe that Jesus died and rose again and so we believe that God will bring with Jesus those who have fallen asleep in him. According to the Lord's own word, we tell you that we who are still alive, who are left till the coming of the Lord, will certainly not precede those who have fallen asleep. For the Lord himself will come down from heaven, with a loud command, with the voice of the archangel and with the trumpet call of God, and the dead in Christ will rise first. After that, we who are still alive and are left will be caught up

together with them in the clouds to meet the Lord in the air. And so
we will be with the Lord forever. Therefore encourage each other
with these words.

If you and I are among the Christians still living when Jesus
returns, we will experience this awesome event, and will ourselves be caught up in the clouds with all the dead in Christ.
What a moment that will be!

And so I agree with the idea of the rapture, to an
extent (more on that in a moment). However, the popular understanding of the tribulation is very wrong. The commonly
accepted view, based on various images from the book of Revelation, is that non-Christians left on earth after the rapture
will experience a time of intense trial in which they suffer at
the hands of the Antichrist, and they will also receive a last
opportunity to repent. But here's the problem with this interpretation: Tribulation (in Greek the word is *thlipsis*) is not
something that happens to non-Christians. Biblically, tribulation is something that happens to Christians. Tribulation
refers to the intense trials that all Christians must endure in
the course of their lives.

However, people have taken Revelation's Technicolor
scenes of judgment and apocalypse—images that are both
metaphorical and somewhat stylized—and morphed them
into a mistaken understanding of the rapture. In so doing,
they have come up with a false doctrine that envisions Christians being raptured up to heaven, where they look down on
the earth and watch as all the non-Christians are punished
and tortured and tested and given a chance to repent. That

concept may make great books and movies, but it is nowhere in the Bible! It has been concocted by combining two disparate elements that have little to do with each other.

Many of the apocalyptic scenes from the book of Revelation are actually referring to God's punishment on the oppressors of the church, the oppressors being the Roman Empire. A full exploration of these ideas is outside the scope of this book, but if you desire more in-depth study, I have produced other material that you may find helpful.[2]

I'm not saying that Revelation has no connection to the end of the world, or that there are no allusions in the book to the ultimate judgment. Of course there are! But most of the prophecies in Revelation have a historical fulfillment that has already occurred—in the first century.

Certainly, the doctrine of the Second Coming is important. But it's not as complex as pop culture would have us believe. The chronology is simple and straightforward: Jesus will come back and call Christians to leave the grave (John 5:22-30), then he will take us to be with him (John 14), and then we will go to heaven. That only happens after the Second Coming.

The Resurrection Body

Many people have questions about what happens to our bodies at the Second Coming. We know we will rise to be with Jesus in heaven, but what form will we take? How, exactly, do Christians resurrect?

We have already discussed this to some extent, in chapter two. You will recall that the Gnostics were false teachers who said that the body was worthless—a shell, a corpse, a prison for the soul—something to be escaped as soon as possible.

My readers who hail from the Protestant stream of thinking may appreciate my own history and the evolution of my thoughts on this topic. When I was at divinity school, I once got into a heated argument with another seminarian, who was Catholic. Predictably, I was not going to agree with him on a number of things. But there was one thing I argued with him about, and only years later did I realize that I was dead wrong.

My classmate claimed that our physical body will be resurrected, and I disagreed. I was defending the traditional view that the soul just goes straight to heaven. But—it gets worse!—I said that the body is corrupt, and so whatever the biblical idea of the "resurrection body" means, it certainly does not refer to our physical body; I insisted that the "resurrection body" is merely a spiritual idea. My Catholic friend asked me to explain what I meant by a spiritual resurrection body, but I couldn't put it into words. I couldn't define it. That should have tipped me off that I was wrong!

Paul is very clear that we are physically resurrected when he discusses the resurrection in 1 Corinthians 15. But he is also clear that Jesus was the firstfruits of the resurrection. Remember that when Jesus rose from the dead, his resurrected body seemed to be the same as the body he had before he died—it even had scars from his crucifixion (John 20:24-30). And although there was some continuity in his physical appearance, there seemed to be some discontinuity as well—some things were apparently different. Sometimes people recognized Jesus, but often they didn't. And I don't think Jesus ever walked through closed doors in his earthly body, but in his resurrected body, he walked through doors (John 20:26, Luke 24:36). He also vanished (Luke 24:31).

An analogy that helps me understand this idea is the acorn and the oak. We know that if an acorn is planted in the ground and given enough time, it will become an oak tree. But imagine if you had never seen a tree before. If someone handed you an acorn and asked you to draw what you believed would grow out of it over time, I seriously doubt that you would draw a sapling, let alone a mighty oak tree! But Paul argues in 1 Corinthians 15 that the body is planted and it grows, like a kind of seed.

In my argument with the seminarian, I committed the classic Protestant mistake: I undervalued the physical body. My Catholic friend was absolutely right: Our physical bodies are raised in the resurrection, but they are different. There's continuity and there's discontinuity. Nevertheless, God gives us all a body, and he has our spirits localized in a body, and that's very important. When Jesus resurrects us at the Second Coming, we will still have some version of the body we now have.

Cremation

I realize that this understanding of the resurrection makes many people nervous, because in their family or culture they cremate loved ones instead of burying them. They worry that the body cannot be resurrected if it has been destroyed.

But I actually don't have a problem with cremation. This issue has come up a number of times in my own family when family members have died and other relatives have asked me if I think it's okay to cremate them. I actually think it is. Let me quote from Tatian, who lived in the 100s. This was written in about 160 AD:

> Even though fire may destroy all traces of my flesh, the world still receives the vaporized matter; and though dispersed through rivers and seas, torn in pieces by wild beasts, I am laid up in the storehouses of the wealthy Lord.[3]

Tatian had no problem with the body being burned, vaporized or eaten. He was not worried, because he put his trust in the Lord. Now it is true that early Christians usually buried their dead, whereas the pagans tended to burn them. But I don't think that's because the Christians thought that if they burned the corpse it could not be resurrected because there would be nothing to resurrect; I think it was more out of respect for the body, because they believed the body was good, not evil. They respected the body as the creation of God.

Athenagoras, writing in AD 175, mentions that, even if a multitude of animals ate your body, it wouldn't prevent the Lord from resurrecting it.[4]

I also find this quotation from Minucius Felix, writing in AD 200, especially helpful:

Do you think that, if anything is withdrawn from our feeble eyes, it perishes to God? Every body, whether it is dried up into dust or is dissolved into moisture, or is compressed into ashes, or is attenuated into smoke, is withdrawn from us, but it is reserved for God in the custody of the elements.[5]

So Minucius Felix apparently didn't have any problem with God's ability to resurrect bodies that had been completely destroyed.

Let me just share a couple more quotations. In AD 180, Irenaeus wrote:

Our bodies, being nourished by [the Eucharist], and deposited in the earth, and suffering decomposition there shall rise at their appointed time, for the Word of God granting them resurrection to the glory of God even the Father, who freely gives to this mortal immortality.[6]

Irenaeus is saying that even if our bodies are decomposed, God will be the one who gives them the glorious resurrection.

And then Tertullian writes this, around AD 197, discussing the general resurrection:

If the flesh is to be repaired after its dissolution, much more will it be restored after some violent injury.[7]

Again, Irenaeus says that even if our bodies are destroyed or decomposed, God can bring them back to life. He goes on to say this:

Much more will it be restored after some violent injury. Greater cases prescribe rules for lesser ones. Is not the amputation or the crushing of a limb the death of that limb? Now, if the death of the whole person is rescinded by its resurrection, what must we say of the death of a part of him?...Thus, for a dead man to be raised again, amounts to nothing short of his being restored to his entire condition, lest he, forsooth, still be dead in that part in which he has not risen again. God is quite able to remake what He once made.[8]

In other words, what's a bigger miracle: to resurrect something that God has already made, or to start from scratch? The bigger miracle was bringing human life in the first place.

People who believe that Christians become angels when they die have trouble with this concept of a resurrected earthly body. But consider Jesus' words in Matthew 22:30: "At the resurrection people will neither marry nor be given in marriage; they will be like the angels in heaven." Note that Jesus says we will be *like* the angels, but we will not *become* angels. There's a big difference! I mentioned in chapter one that when I was a child, people told me that people become angels when they die. Presumably, angels do not have bodies like ours, which would change our view of the way God resurrects us. But Jesus only says we will be *like* the angels. So in the resurrected body, we will still be ourselves, but we will have a glorified body.

The Nature of Judgment

All of this centers around the final judgment at the end of times. Let's review by summarizing three basic facts about the judgment: First, the judgment is declarative, not investigative. Second, our ultimate judgment is already decided at the point we die. And third, there is no second chance. (And that means there is no reincarnation and no purgatory.)

The simplicity in the understanding is this: Everyone on the planet will be judged at the same time, both the righteous and the wicked. John 5:28-29 informs us that all will be judged on the same day. How could that be true if the saints are already in heaven?

As we have established, the saved await judgment in paradise, consciously and happily, while the damned wait in the punishing part of Hades (sometimes called Tartarus) until the Judgment Day. So everyone is judged at the same time. We may think that God decides our ultimate fate only after the Judgment Day, because in a human court of law, the judge does not decide the guilt or innocence of a prisoner before hearing the evidence. But this is where the analogy breaks down, because God, the righteous Judge, is not like earthly judges. "The Judge of all the earth," as Abraham describes him in Genesis 18:25, does not need inquiry or evidence. He is omniscient, and so he already knows all about us. This means that when we die, our fate is sealed.

And so the Judgment Day at the end of time will not be an investigation; it will be a declaration. God won't be examining the records of our lives in a courtroom scene to see if we've made it. Rather, he'll declare our final destiny. At that point, the righteous will be escorted into the glory of heaven, while the wicked will be cast into the lake of fire.

Those who loved God during their days on earth will

be saved forever, while those who rejected God will be destroyed. And as we have shown, there's no second chance after death. There is no purgatory. We only have one chance to get things right—let's live our lives in light of the day of judgment, with reverence and zeal for God—and look forward with confidence to the day when our Father welcomes us into heaven to dwell with him forever.

Chapter 5

Jesus' Descent into Hades

      I grew up in the Anglican church, and I was confirmed when I was thirteen. To prepare for my confirmation, I had to memorize the Ten Commandments, the Apostles' Creed and the Lord's Prayer. The Apostles' Creed really bothered me because it talked about Jesus going to hell. I didn't really know what to do with that idea, and if you're not familiar with the Apostles' Creed, elements of it trace back to the first or second century. In this modern version, they have taken out the word hell and have translated it more accurately as "the dead":

> I believe in God, the Father almighty,
> creator of heaven and earth.
> I believe in Jesus Christ, his only Son, our Lord.
> He was conceived by the power of the Holy Spirit
> and born of the Virgin Mary,
> He suffered under Pontius Pilate,
> was crucified, died and was buried.

He descended to the dead.
On the third day he rose again.
He ascended into heaven,
and is seated at the right hand of the Father.
He will come again to judge the living and the dead.
I believe in the Holy Spirit,
the holy catholic Church,
the communion of saints,
the forgiveness of sins,
the resurrection of the body,
and the life everlasting.
Amen.[1]

Now there are many truths here we would do well to focus on. Many of us in the biblical and evangelical stream don't talk enough about the resurrection of the body. We don't talk enough about the return of the Lord to judge the living and the dead.

Notice the sequence in this particular creed: Jesus died, was buried, descended to the dead (to Hades), rose, ascended to heaven, is seated at the right hand of God, and he will come again. I think it's important to respect all the great doctrines of the New Testament, but also the sequence of those doctrines.

In a side note, it's interesting to note that the clause about Jesus descending to the dead—to Hades—was omitted from the Nicene Creed.[2] I don't really know why, but it does bring up an interesting question: What did Jesus do between Friday evening, when he died, and Sunday morning, when he resurrected? We find a clue in 1 Peter 3:18-19:

> For Christ also suffered once for sins, the righteous for the unrigh-
> teous, to bring you to God. He was put to death in the body but
> made alive in the Spirit. After being made alive, he went and made
> proclamation to the imprisoned spirits.

If that's not a difficult passage, I don't know what is.
And Peter said that Paul had written some difficult passages!
(2 Peter 3:16). But let's take a closer look. This scripture
says that Jesus was put to death in the flesh and made alive
in the spirit, that he went and made proclamations to the
spirits now in prison. He was put to death in the flesh on the
cross, and that happened on the day we call Good Friday. But
when was he made alive in the spirit? He wasn't made alive
in the body till Sunday. But he was made alive *in the spirit*
right after he died. And the Bible says that he went to the
spirits now in prison and preached to them.

The early Christians had many different ideas about
what this passage meant. Some thought that Jesus spoke to
the spirits in prison and gave them the gospel message, and
if they believed, then they were saved. The "spirits in prison"
were said to be the Old Testament saints, the good people
from the Old Testament.

Other early Christians thought that Jesus spoke to
those who were condemned, but his preaching did not change
anything about their eternal destinies; he simply proved to
them that the truth of God had been vindicated.

Other early believers thought that Jesus went to

Hades and preached, and later, when the apostles died, Jesus preached in Hades again. And if people responded, they baptized them in Hades!

Still others would say that Jesus went into hell and "harrowed" it—that is, he cleaned out Hades. He proclaimed, "I have conquered death," and he led all the spirits in Hades up to heaven. That was a popular idea in the medieval era, but the problem is that again, it bypasses the resurrection and the Judgment Day.

Some scholars think the spirits Jesus spoke to in Hades were angelic, not human. But I'm not convinced of that. Peter suggests only a few verses later that because people must one day give an account for their actions, the gospel has been preached to those who are now dead. This verse refers to people, not angels:

> They think it strange that you do not plunge with them into the same flood of dissipation, and they heap abuse on you. But they will have to give account to him who is ready to judge the living and the dead. For this is the reason the gospel was preached even to those who are now dead, so that they might be judged according to men in regard to the body, but live according to God in regard to the spirit. (1 Peter 4:4–6)

So is Peter saying that the gospel was preached to living people on earth, and *then* they died...or he is saying the gospel was preached to them *after* they died?

I would choose the first answer, except for one problem: the proximity of this passage to 1 Peter 3:18-19, where we learn that Jesus proclaimed to the spirits in prison. It seems to me that this passage supports the early Christian teaching that somehow the gospel message was shared with those who had died. But again, I wish I had more to go on, and I cannot be dogmatic.

Let me tell you what I used to teach. In the 1970s, I heard a preacher say that Jesus preached to the spirits in prison *through Noah*. Again, 1 Peter 3:18-20 reads,

> He was put to death in the body but made alive in the Spirit. After being made alive, he went and made proclamation to the imprisoned spirits—to those who were disobedient long ago when God waited patiently in the days of Noah while the ark was being built. In it only a few people, eight in all, were saved through water.

Now to be fair, the passage doesn't say that Noah shared his faith in God with his friends. That's an inference. His example alone would have been a kind of preaching, but the idea is that he preached. Then you combine that with a thought in 1 Peter 1:10-11 where Peter writes,

> Concerning this salvation, the prophets, who spoke of the grace that was to come to you, searched intently and with the greatest care, trying to find out the time and circumstances to which the Spirit of Christ in them was pointing when he predicted the sufferings of Christ and the glories that would follow.

The passage in 1 Peter 1 says the Spirit of Christ was in the prophets. So if you take Noah as a prophet in 2 Peter 2, you can have Christ preaching through Noah to the wicked of his generation.

That's a pretty persuasive argument, and I like it a lot. The problem is, I just don't think it's true. Something tells me that even though it's attractive, it's wrong. And when I move from 1 Peter into the patristic literature and read what the church fathers wrote, they all seemed to believe that Jesus preached to the dead after his crucifixion and before his resurrection. Therefore, we return to Ephesians 4:8-10:

> "When he [Jesus] ascended on high,
> he led captives in his train
> and gave gifts to men."
> (What does "he ascended" mean except that he also descended
> to the lower, earthly regions? He who descended is the very one
> who ascended higher than all the heavens, in order to fill the whole
> universe.)

The reference to filling the universe, in my mind, is a reference to the tripartite universe.

All this indicates that the doctrine of Jesus' descent to Hades is part of the ancient Christian teaching, which I'm afraid we've lost over time.

Having said that, we should be clear on one thing: The souls that Jesus preached to did not receive a second chance at attaining salvation. The Bible never says that these spirits got a chance to repent. That would contradict Hebrews 9:27, where it says, "Just as man is destined to die once, and after that to face judgment."

If your head is spinning a bit at this point, that's okay. When we dive deep into the waters of biblical teaching, we sometimes get dizzied by the pressure change! Theologians have been debating these complex topics for years, and the many theories are difficult to compress into a short book. I urge you to continue your study of these subjects—to read other books; to explore and weigh different viewpoints. And in the end, I hope the "pressure" you experience from expanding your thinking and deepening your Bible knowledge will enrich your experience of the Bible, intensify your walk with God, and encourage you in your pursuit of heaven.

Chapter 6

What Will We Do in Heaven?

Let's briefly revisit the Garden of Eden, which we mentioned in chapter one, and explore how it relates to and informs our view of the afterlife. I provide a detailed exploration of the Garden of Eden and its connection to paradise in my book *Genesis, Science and History*.[1] But remember that the Septuagint (the Greek translation of the Old Testament) regularly uses the word *paradeisos* for garden, not just in Genesis 2–3, but in other books of the Bible as well (see chart below).

The Use of *Paradeisos* in the Old Testament

Numbers 24:6–"Like valleys they spread out, like *gardens* beside a river"
Ecclesiastes 2:5–"I made *gardens* and parks..."
Song of Songs 4:13–"Your plants are an *orchard* of pomegranates"
Isaiah 1:30–"...like a *garden* without water"
Isaiah 51:3–"The Lord will surely comfort Zion...like the *gardens* of the Lord"
Ezekiel 28:13–"You were in Eden, the *garden* of God"
Ezekiel 31:8–"The cedars in the *garden* of God..."
Ezekiel 31:9–"...the envy of all the trees of Eden in the *garden* of God"
Ezekiel 36:35–"This land...has become like the *garden* of Eden..."

Between Two Paradises

Some have noted that biblical history depicts human history as framed by two paradises. But these are paradises in two different senses of the word. We have the original paradise on earth, the Garden of Eden. But at the end of time, we all have the opportunity to stop over in paradise on our way to heaven. What we do with our life in between the two paradises (and whether we get to go to paradise when we die!) is up to us.

Now let's talk more specifically about heaven. What will it be like? What will we do there?

What Heaven Is

Heaven is the very presence of God. Heaven is our ultimate reward. Most religions envision a place of reward, a heaven of some kind. In other religions, heaven is sometimes called paradise (to use the other sense of the word), while hell is viewed as a place of punishment.

Popular Hinduism has millions of hells and heavens. Similarly, Buddhism, which originally held an atheistic worldview, eventually created many heavens and many hells. Modern Buddhism (just like Islam, Catholicism and other religions) has evolved away from its origins. It seems that even when the intellectual members of a religion deny the truth about the existence of an afterlife, the people reconstruct it, almost by popular emotional demand. Buddha said, in so many words, "There's no heaven and there's no hell; there's no you and there's no self, and there's no God." But people can't live that way. So not only did Buddha's followers create the heavens and the hells and God and the gods, they also made Buddha a god, the last thing he wanted.

There is something in the spiritual heart of man that knows that the evil deserve punishment, while the righteous deserve reward. And this is not salvation by works; it's justice, it's right, it's fair, it's biblically correct.

What Heaven Isn't

Let's say a few things about what heaven is not. First, it's not an amusement park or a sensual pleasure palace; it's not the so-called "garden or paradise" of Islam or Hinduism or other religions. In man-made religions, heaven is the place where sin becomes acceptable. In fact, a Muslim man who abstains from sin in his earthly life is *rewarded* in paradise with the very sins he abstained from! Consider the well-known citation from Sura 37:40-41 in the *Qur'an*, the Muslim scriptures:

> The true servants of Allah will be well provided for, feasting on fruit and honored in the gardens of delight. Reclining face to face upon soft couches, they shall be served with a goblet filled at a gushing fountain, white, and delicious to those who drink it. They shall sit with bashful, dark-eyed virgins, as chaste as the sheltered eggs of ostriches.

Here you get the idea that the true servants who will receive reward in heaven are men, and women will only be there as servants. In popular Islam, it is taught that if you die for the faith, you will get as many as seventy virgins just for yourself.

Sura 78:29 offers "high-bosomed maidens" for the men who persevere—high-bosomed maidens whom neither man nor genie would have touched on earth! This is nothing more than a natural, humanistic way of envisioning heaven. And it's very attractive...if you're a man. We find in these writings both a strong appeal to ego and libido: Eat and drink to your heart's content!

But this concept of heaven is not unique to Islam. The Vikings had their Valhalla, the banquet hall of the god Odin. This was where the Valkyrie maidens waited on the warriors as they feasted each night. Vikings believed that in the afterlife, you would fight in the day and feast at night. As one writer put it, Valhalla was not the only paradise that provided escort services for its male clientele. The Celts had a land of the women; the medieval Germans had the ambiguous Venusberg; and we've already mentioned how the Muslims have the dark-eyed houries.

But I assure you that heaven is not a pleasure palace. That idea is vastly inferior to the wonder of fellowshipping with God.

Secondly, heaven is not a place of lethargy. Many people think that when we get to heaven, we will lie around with nothing to do, resting in hammocks. Even in the first paradise, in Eden, God had work for man to do (Genesis 2:15). He put Adam and Eve there to take care of the Garden, even before the entrance of sin into the world.

So work itself is not a punishment. From the very beginning, there was work and responsibility and dominion in the Garden of Eden. As humans, we were created to be busy, to be active; to function with a certain level of pressure and intensity. And if we don't work in some way, we are not fulfilled. I enjoy hard work, and recreation is never more rewarding than when I know I've poured myself out for what's worthwhile. You know what I mean, don't you? When you've worked hard, then rest is all the more sweet. Sports and games, in the same way, are more fun when the competition is more intense (to a point!). Idleness and laziness are corrupting influences—do we really think that things will somehow be different in heaven? Certainly we will be less influenced by the corrosive influence of idleness, but will that mean that we have nothing to do? Is it not more reasonable to suppose that God has work for us to do that he's been training us for during our time on earth?

But many of us have such a lame, boring concept of heaven that we end up inventing colorful analogies in a desperate attempt to make heaven sound more desirable. We imagine a place where we can eat mountains of sumptuous foods without expanding the waistline, or a place where we can fly or accomplish superhuman feats, or participate in incredible adventures. The more intellectually inclined among us may conceive of heaven as a library stocked with scintillating reading. But in fact, none of these fantasies hold a candle to the real thing.

What Will We Be Like in Heaven?

Many people assume that we will be omniscient in heaven. I often hear people say, "Well, I'll have to ask the

Lord about that when I get to heaven," or, "I'll ask Paul what he meant when he wrote that." Or, "You know I'll be able to understand quantum physics in heaven. I'll just ask the Creator and he will explain it to me." I'm not so sure that I'd understand quantum physics even if the Creator himself sat me down and taught me!

We are not promised omniscience as part of a salvation package deal. We will become like Christ in some ways (1 John 3:2), but that doesn't mean we're going to have all knowledge and become God. That's an eastern, pantheistic interpretation of heaven.

What Will We Do in Heaven?

So again we ask: What is heaven, and what will we do there? First of all, heaven is a reward. It's a fellowship with our God. It's a rest, and yet there'll be activity. We will enjoy the fulfillment of performing work entrusted to us by our Father—only in heaven, our work will not be frustrated as it is here on earth (see Genesis 3:17-19). All our needs will be met. We won't be troubled by bad memories, fleshly temptations, nagging doubts, or aching muscles. After the exhaustion and trouble we face in life on earth, we won't be weary anymore. We will need a break, and heaven will be that break. It will also be a fresh start.

What Does Revelation Tell Us (and NOT Tell Us) About Heaven?

The many metaphors in Revelation 21 and 22 are commonly understood to be describing heaven, and many people have used them to create a concept of heaven that is not entirely biblical. But strictly speaking, those passages describe the church triumphant, the church delivered from the Roman persecution. Let's briefly explore this idea, because misapplication of the metaphors in Revelation has led to a number of misunderstandings about heaven and the afterlife. Not everyone agrees with my interpretation of these passages, but allow me to pose a few questions.

If Revelation 21 refers primarily to heaven, why does the new Jerusalem come down from heaven in Revelation 21:2? In other words, if it *is* heaven, why does it come *out* of heaven, *down from* heaven to the earth? If it's heaven, how come the Gentiles (the nations) are still on the earth (21:26)? Why do they require healing (22:2), and who are these people who dwell outside the city of God anyway? And 21:24 says their kings will bring their splendor into the new Jerusalem. These questions don't go away by insisting even louder that the passage must be talking about heaven! I agree that it does refer indirectly to heaven. Revelation talks about heaven and hell, but not necessarily in this passage, and it certainly doesn't tell us all there is to know about heaven. It's not quite that simple.

Of course, it's impossible to read Revelation and not think about heaven and the new order of things. To get a glimpse of heaven and hell, it is appropriate to extend these metaphors beyond the time of John and the cessation of persecution, all the way to the end of time. We see from Revelation and many other passages that heaven will be magnificent, a place where "glory, honor and immortality" will be the nonstop elements of our very existence (Romans 2:7). Revelation does point to heaven, but it doesn't describe or explain it fully. I would therefore urge caution as you read Revelation. It is an apocalyptic book rife with intense imagery and symbolism, and the wise reader will do their homework before pulling images out of Revelation and applying them willy-nilly to a patchwork theology of the afterlife.

I would encourage you to also read everything that Jesus says about judgment and the afterlife to add to your understanding of heaven. Jesus spoke often about heaven, and he used human analogies to help us understand what a joyful place it will be. He compared it to a banquet, a wedding, and to his Father's home—all positive, exciting analogies that help us look forward to what God has in store for those who love him.

What, then, is heaven? It is reward, it is rest, it is eternity with the Father who loves us. It is a feast, a celebration, a home. It is the place where the evils of this limited life and the shortcomings of this fallen world are overcome at last. It is far superior to the shallow, chauvinistic, humanistic "heavens" that other religions imagine. And while some of heaven's characteristics remain mysterious (and personally, I find that a little mystery piques my interest and keeps me excited about the future!), we can be confident that our future home will be "immeasurably more than all we ask or imagine" (Ephesians 3:20), and that there is nowhere else we'd rather be.

As for me...I don't know all there is to know about

heaven, but I do know this: I want to go there one day, and I'm determined to live my life in such a way that God, through his grace and the gift of his Son, will welcome me in. My prayer for all of us is that one day we all enter the gates of heaven and hear those long-awaited words: "Well done, good and faithful servant. Come and share in your master's happiness" (Matthew 25:21).

Chapter 7

What to Do with
What You've Learned

Perhaps by now your head is spinning a bit, trying to take all of this in, to reorient your thoughts and expectations about the afterlife. I realize that some of these ideas are foreign, maybe even a bit frightening, if you've never heard them before. And so I offer you a few thoughts on what to do with these new ideas.

To start, please don't be surprised if you have not heard these concepts before; don't be surprised if the tradition of teaching you've received is wrong. There are a lot of things from our received tradition that are wrong–teachings that we inherited from the medieval church like infant baptism and the idea of clergy and laity. If so many other popular teachings are in error, why should it surprise us that the modern teaching of what happens after death is also wrong, or at least incomplete?

Now remember, the idea of an intermediate state for the dead hasn't been completely lost. Some groups still teach it correctly. In another sense, it was never completely lost anyway, because it was always right there in the Bible! But even if no church or preacher anywhere were teaching it, you and I would still have to accept what the Scriptures say.

Hold on to Humility

But at the same time, please use your new knowledge to help, not harm. After reading this book, it might be tempting to look down upon people who have never been exposed to the correct doctrine. We have all been taught many things incorrectly, and have even taught others biblical "truths" that we later reevaluated. So let's not throw around the label "false teacher" too quickly. Let's not be arrogant, because we all need the grace of God, even in biblical interpretations. Rather, let's recommit ourselves to searching the Scriptures.

Hold on to Hope

Perhaps the idea of going to paradise on your way to heaven has made you feel unsettled, unsure, or less excited about the afterlife. But let me assure you: You have everything to look forward to. Remember that even though we are not going to heaven but to the intermediate state (unless we live in the last generation, of course!), we still have assurance that after death we are "at home with the Lord," as Paul put it (2 Corinthians 5:8). Dying in the Lord means dying saved. It doesn't mean going immediately to heaven, although we will go to heaven someday. In the meantime, we will enjoy the comfort of the Lord in the place called Abraham's bosom, or paradise. It will be wonderful. This is in no way less thrilling than the old doctrine of dying and going straight to heaven. In fact, if anything, paradise increases suspense and it whets our appetite. It prepares us through an intermediate step for something that will be nearly completely overwhelming when we do finally experience it.

Hold on to Truth

You may have heard these clever words of Winston Churchill: "Most people, sometime in their lives, stumble across truth. Most jump up, brush themselves off, and hurry about their business as if nothing had happened."

Isn't that so true? In fact, don't we all do that? But let's not do that when it comes to the Bible. Rather, let's study what the Bible says. Let's be good Bereans, who "received the message with great eagerness and examined the Scriptures every day to see if what Paul said was true" (Acts 17:11). Let's not just swallow a teaching because it seems pleasant. Let's swallow it because it's true, because it's faithful to the Scriptures—because that's the real question, isn't it?

But let's not search only the Scriptures. I urge you to also read other things. The patristic writings and the teachings of the early church are immensely helpful and illuminate many biblical doctrines. I've already suggested that you take advantage of the ministry of David Berçot, a man who has devoted his life to bringing the patristic writings to the attention of the general public. Among many other helpful books you could read, I recommend F. LaGard Smith's *Afterlife*[1] as well as my own *What's the Truth About Heaven and Hell?*[2]—assuming you want to go into significantly more depth on the issues surrounding the afterlife.

I encourage you to push yourself, to expand your thinking. Don't only read books written by people you already agree with, and don't only read books written by people "in our camp." If you want to put on muscle, you've got to work your muscles; you've got to stretch them. You've got to challenge yourself. So let me encourage you to search the Scriptures first and foremost, but also to go beyond the Scriptures to supplement your study.

Prepare for Heaven

But most important, let's prepare ourselves for death. It would be a tragedy if we figured out what could happen after death and embraced the biblical doctrine of Hades, but still ended up not going to heaven. If we discover the truth about the afterlife but are not actually prepared to die, that would be the worst irony of all. So let's prepare ourselves. Let's not be caught off-guard like the rich fool in Luke 12, and let's keep in mind the words of Jesus in Luke 18:8: "When the Son of Man comes, will he find faith on the earth?" I hope, in your case and in mine, that he will find faith in our hearts. Once we die and enter the intermediate state of the dead, there is no chance of altering our eternal destiny. That possibility exists only while we are here on earth, in the body, still alive.

Then, provided we're not living in the last generation of human beings, we will hear his voice at the last trumpet call, rise from the dead in our resurrection bodies, and approach the very throne of God. For God has set a day. He has set a day when, in his wisdom, he will bring all mankind before his throne to be pronounced guilty or innocent. And at that time, we will fully receive our reward. May God bless you as you continue to study this important theme and as you prepare for life after death.

Appendix

Heaven and Hell: Terminal Punishment

Explaining my view of eternal punishment

Introduction

In my view, hell doesn't last infinitely, but instead destroys the individual after an appropriate length of time. Hell is eternal in its consequences, not in its duration. "Terminal punishment" describes this view. Any length of time in hell that is less than infinite implies the terminal view. This is in contrast to the traditional view, which holds that the individual is tormented endlessly in the fire of hell. In other words, God prolongs one's life infinitely for the purpose of punishment.

If you conceive of eternal punishment as lasting millions and millions of years—but still ending at some point—you are in basic agreement with my thesis. (Even five hundred million years, as long as that may seem, is virtually *nothing* in comparison with infinite time.) *Any* amount of time less than forever (infinity) implies the *terminal* view, as the following table illustrates. In the next world (in what we call eternity) we may be entering a timeless state which defies chronological analysis. Nevertheless, the table may be a useful tool.

TIME AND ETERNITY

Time in hell	View of punishment
None (instantly extinguished)	Annihilationist
One million years	Terminal
One week	Terminal
One year	Terminal
Ten days	Terminal
One second	Terminal
Eight and one half minutes	Terminal
Two years	Terminal
Five hundred billion years	Terminal
Four hours	Terminal
Seven trillion years	Terminal
Seven trillion centuries	Terminal
Seven trillion millennia	Terminal
Infinite time	Traditional

I hope the difference between traditional and terminal understandings is clear. The terminal view is simply that after a period of torment ("corporal punishment") suited to the individual, God destroys him/her ("capital punishment"). The distinction can also be understood by the following paradigm:

Traditional view:	(Infinite) corporal punishment
Annihilationist view:	Capital punishment
Terminal view:	Corporal + capital punishment

In addition to terminal punishment, I also hold that the soul of a man is not eternal. Immortality is a gift only for the saved. These two doctrines—the mortality of the soul and the finite nature of hell—are central to the terminal view of hell.

The right attitude

I realize many disciples sincerely hold to the traditional position, while a number have been persuaded to the terminal view. At this point there's no consensus, though a show of hands might result in the triumph of the traditional view. But truth isn't determined by show of hands or popular referendum. What's needed is a thorough study of the issue. We need to study what the inspired word of God says. My aim is not a dogmatic pronouncement on the subject (Acts 15-style), but rather a diligent search into the truth of the matter. The issue isn't what *feels* right, or what *works* best, but what the truth is. I hope the paper is helpful to you as you study the matter for yourself.

I. OBJECTIONS CONSIDERED

Let's be a little unorthodox and consider some of the objections before we even develop the thesis. This is helpful because of the emotionally loaded nature of any discussion on eternal punishment. Preconceptions eventually need to be addressed. (As long as the person has "the sinner's prayer" or "the thief on the cross" in the back of his mind as an objection to getting baptized, you'll be limited in your ability to persuade him. Show him there's another feasible interpretation, and his mind opens up to the possibility.) The question is, "Is it even *possible* to consider another view of hell?"

A. Jesus' words in Mark 9

What about Jesus' own words on hell? Jesus is in fact the Bible's main spokesman on the subject. Do his words refute the terminal view, or is there another logical way to look at the subject?

If your hand causes you to stumble, cut it off. It is better for you to enter life maimed than with two hands to go into hell, where the fire never goes out.

And if your foot causes you to stumble, cut it off. It is better for you to enter life crippled than to have two feet and be thrown into hell. And if your eye causes you to stumble, pluck it out. It is better for you to enter the kingdom of God with one eye than to have two eyes and be thrown into hell, where 'their worm does not die, and the fire is not quenched.' Everyone will be salted with fire." (Mark 9:43–49)

Mark 9 seems to imply that the wicked will forever burn in the fire of hell. Similarly, John 3:16 seems to support salvation by faith alone. After all, it states that "whoever *believes* in him shall not perish." But then Luke 13:5, supplying additional information, shows that we must *repent* in order not to perish. Surprisingly, a closer look at Mark 9 hardly proves that the wicked burn forever and ever. The Old Testament quotation at the end of the passage turns out to be a direct citation from Isaiah.

Notice that Mark 9 doesn't explicitly say *people* in hell are undying. (The only "immortal" creatures in the passage are the worms!) And anyway, an eternal fire wouldn't logically necessitate that whatever is thrown into it would burn eternally, only that the fire wouldn't go out. Whatever is thrown into that fire would sooner or later be completely burned up. It's a *consuming* fire. Likewise the "unquenchable fire" of Jeremiah 17:27; it does *not* burn forever, though the destruction it wreaks is certainly serious and thorough. Let's carefully consider the Isaiah passage which Jesus cites:

All mankind will come and bow down before me," says the Lord. "And they will go out and look upon the dead bodies of those who rebelled against me; their worm will not die, nor will their fire be quenched, and they will be loathsome to all mankind. (Isaiah 66:23–24)

What does this passage, borrowed by Jesus to illustrate the nature of hell, really teach?

- The bodies are dead, not living. They're unconscious.
- They are those who rebelled against God.
- They are being consumed by worms and fire.
- The scene evokes feelings of disgust, not pity.

Whether we should take the immortality of the worms literally is certainly questionable. But the thrust of the passage is clear enough: the rebels have been destroyed. They aren't conscious. They feel no pain. Furthermore, the emotional panorama is different to the one conjured up by the traditional view. The sight is disgusting. No feelings of *pity* are welling up, only loathing and *disgust*. After all, they're dead and decaying.

Has Jesus perhaps changed the original meaning of the passage? The burden of proof is on the traditional view, which Isaiah 66 and Mark 9, when read *naturally*, do not convincingly support. There certainly seems to be a case for the terminal view here. I'm not asking you to accept the new view just yet, only to admit that the objection from Mark 9 isn't conclusive. Isaiah 66 may well speak against the traditional view.

We may assume everyone in Jesus' day understood him to mean *infinite* torment. But the support for this is weaker than we may think. It comes primarily from the Apocrypha. The first time the Apocrypha (c.200 BC–AD 110) speaks of eternal torment is in the book of Judith, written approximately 125 BC:

Woe to the nations that rise up against my people! The Lord Almighty will take vengeance on them in the day of judgment; he will send fire and worms into their flesh; they shall weep in pain for ever. (Judith 16:17, RSV)

Biblical Words Concerning Eternity

Word	Language	Definition
Aion	Greek	Age *(aion)*: a segment or period of time
Aionios	Greek	Eternal; relating to an *aion*; No necessary implication of infinity
Aevum	Latin	Age—same as Greek *aion*
Aeternus	Latin	Lasting, eternal
'Olam	Hebrew	Age, period of time, forever

Whereas Isaiah's fire and worms destroy the individual, Judith's fire and worms torture. What a contrast! This is the one clear passage in support of the traditional view from the Apocrypha. Other Apocryphal passages on the subject support the view that the wicked will be destroyed, *not* tormented forever. Even the later pseudepigrapha has a mixed witness on this subject, some passages in favor of the later view, others favoring the traditional view. The Dead Sea Scrolls, from the two centuries before Christ, unanimously teach the extinction of the wicked.

To be fair, it should be admitted that some patristic writers (church fathers in the first few centuries after Christ) do follow Judith, but we must remember that (1) their writings date from after the close of the New Testament canon, (2) Jesus gives no credence to the (Old Testament) apocryphal writings, and (3) these books lack biblical authority, since we can hardly decide our views based on extra-biblical sources.

B. The meaning of "eternal" in Matthew 25

If it can be shown that "eternal" is used in more than one way, then there's a case for the terminal view. But *can* it in fact be taken in only one way?

The familiar conclusion to the parable of the sheep and

goats reads, "Then they will go away to eternal punishment, but the righteous to eternal life." At first inspection the passage seems to support the traditional view strongly. The reasoning is simple: If the eternal life lasts forever, then the eternal punishment must last equally long. Therefore hell is forever. Settled! And that does sound logical.

Alas, there are good reasons to reject this interpretation. To begin with, it doesn't fit well with Mark 9, if our analysis above is correct. The first passage assumes that consciousness has ceased; the other, it is alleged, assumes consciousness is unending. Then there's a logical problem. *Why* would someone be tortured *forever* in hell for sins committed during a *limited* period of time on earth? God rewards to the *thousandth* generation, but punishes only to the *third* or *fourth* (Exodus 20:5-6). This is the Bible's own commentary on the unchanging character of God (Malachi 3:6). But the most important argument against the traditional view of Matthew 25 is the evidence from Jude. Yes, the little letter of Jude, brother of Jesus.

> In a similar way, Sodom and Gomorrah and the surrounding towns gave themselves up to sexual immorality and perversion. They serve as an example of those who suffer the punishment of eternal fire. (Jude 7)

Go back to Genesis 19. Or go to the geographical area of Sodom and Gomorrah. Did the combustion continue after the fire and brimstone fell? Is it still burning today? So how exactly were they "an example of those who suffer the punishment of *eternal* fire"? Is Jude confused? (And was Peter confused in 2 Peter 2:6?)

Actually, in the Scriptures, Sodom and Gomorrah are the prototype of those who suffer God's wrath and punishment (Genesis 19:24-29; Lamentations 4:6; Deuteronomy 29:22-24; Amos 4:11; Isaiah 1:9; Zephaniah 2:9; Isaiah 13:19-22; Luke 17:28-29;

Jeremiah 49:18, 50:40; 2 Peter 2:6). Yet in every one of these cases, as with the original (Sodom), the punishment is limited in duration!

Now back to the question of the meaning of "eternal" in Matthew 25:46. How could hell be eternal *without* lasting forever? It could be eternal *in its effects*. The result of punishment is total, irreversible, eternal. In eternity the verdict will forever read the same. Before reacting against this interpretation of the word "eternal" as special pleading, consider several passages that are apropos:

Hebrews 6:2 speaks of **"eternal judgment."** Is the process of judging itself eternal, or only the consequence, the sentence? It's obvious in this verse "eternal" is being used to describe the effects, *not* the act of judging itself. (Incidentally, eternal judgment, which is the subject of this paper, is one of the "elementary teachings." All the more reason to figure this out.)

Mark 3:29 mentions an **"eternal sin."** Its guilt will never be forgiven. But it isn't the sin itself (as an action) that's eternal. The sin isn't committed forever and ever, but the results of the sin are everlasting. It will never be forgiven.

Hebrews 9:12 speaks of the **"eternal redemption"** that Christ has affected. Hebrews, of all New Testament books, makes it clear that the redeeming itself is a once-for-all event. So we're speaking of the results or consequences of the redemption Jesus Christ has purchased for us. His atoning death is over; now he is resurrected and at the right hand of the Father. What can we conclude from these three passages?

- In all three cases above the word "eternal" is *not* used in the usual, more familiar way. So "eternal" can be understood in more than one way.

- In Matthew 25:46 there's no compelling reason to take "eternal" in the traditional way. The language and interpretational possibilities don't demand it.
- Jude 7 supports the terminal view against the traditional view.

Matthew 25 by no means forces us to accept the traditional view! We have to let the Bible define its terms. In the case of the word "eternal," we must determine whether biblical writers and speakers mean eternal in the sense of *a continuous action or state*, or eternal in the sense of a *consequence or result*. In addition, there are a number of scriptures where words such as "forever," "eternal," and "everlasting" do not necessarily entail a sense of *infinite duration*. For example, the following list is based (only) on the Greek root *aion**, which appears in the LXX and the New Testament numerous times, with the general sense of (world) age, forever, always, eternity, etc. In none of the following cases does the word *aion** bear the sense of infinite eternity.

- Genesis 6:4–"Men of old" (giants/ungodly persons/fallen ones/sons of Cain) did not live infinitely
- Jeremiah 25:12–Destruction of Babylon (though not literally destroyed)
- Genesis 9:12–Perpetual generations
- Exodus 21:6–The man or woman would become one's servant "forever" (!)
- Leviticus 25:34–Perpetual possession of fields
- Deuteronomy 23:3–"Forever"–the 10th generation
- 1 Samuel 1:22–Young Samuel was to serve at the house of the Lord "forever"
- 1 Chronicles 16:15–"Forever"–1000 generations–also Psalm 105:8

- Ezra 4:15,19–Israelites had been "eternally" resisting political domination
- Psalm 24:7–"Ancient" doors
- Proverbs 22:28–"Ancient" boundary stone
- Jonah 2:6–Prophet confined in (the fish) "forever"

C. Revelation 14 and 20

Before I tackle a few objections from Revelation, let me encourage us to exercise caution when interpreting this highly figurative "book of prophecy" (Revelation 22:19). Many false doctrines have been fabricated from its verses, and we need to tread carefully. In my view it is impossible to take this book literally. By "literally" I don't mean "seriously" or "at face value"! The book must be taken seriously, as both warnings and blessings are attached to reading it in chapters 1 and 22. But actually much of the Bible is impossible to take "literally": apocalyptic, a good deal of prophecy, many figures of speech, accommodative language, many Psalms and other poetry... The rule of thumb when reading Revelation is: **Take the passage figuratively unless forced to do otherwise**, because literal interpretation almost always does violence to the text. (For example, consider the 144,000 in heaven of Revelation 7 and 14, who strictly speaking are celibate Jewish males only.)

Revelation has immediate application to the Roman Empire, which was just commencing its severe persecution of the Christians in the reign of Domitian, the Caesar from AD 81-96. In Revelation 22:14 we read of people both inside and outside the city, but from 22:11 and 22:2 it's quite clear there were still many non-Christians (those "outside") carrying on life as normal. This is *after* the New Jerusalem has come down! (In contrast to the common view that takes the book, especially its final chapters, to describe some future state.) There's a lot we can glean from Revelation, yet we must glean ever so carefully.

There are two passages problematic for the terminal view. If they're taken at face value there are certainly some questions to answer.

> A third angel followed them and said in a loud voice: "If anyone worships the beast and his image and receives his mark on the forehead or on the hand, he, too, will drink of the wine of God's fury, which has been poured full strength into the cup of his wrath. He will be tormented with burning sulfur in the presence of the holy angels and of the Lamb. And the smoke of their torment rises for ever and ever. There is no rest day or night for those who worship the beast and his image, or for anyone who receives the mark of his name." (Revelation 14:9–11)

While a cursory reading might lead you to think that this ongoing torment is "for all eternity," there are several reasons to discount that interpretation. The passage is specific to the time of the Roman Empire, and the language highly figurative. The smoke is eternal, but not explicitly the torment. That may be our conclusion, but the passage doesn't state it. "No rest day or night" may just as well imply a limited period of time as an eternal one.

These passages from Revelation are especially helpful:

> When they see the smoke of her burning, they will exclaim, "Was there ever a city like this great city?" (Revelation 18:18)

> And again they shouted: "Hallelujah! The smoke from her goes up for ever and ever!" (Revelation 19:3)

These passages describe the destruction of Rome, imperial headquarters of the persecuting power and enemy of the faithful. Notice the words "for ever and ever," which emphasize not the duration of the smoke or burning but the permanence of the destruction. The careful reader will note that the "smoke of her burning" (18:9) is the result of her being "consumed by fire" (18:8), the just punishment for her sin (18:6-7). In this case punishment was proportional and finite, not infinite in duration.

This has Old Testament parallels. Isaiah 34:10 speaks of the destruction of Edom: "It will not be quenched night and day; its smoke will rise forever." Edom was laid waste centuries before Christ, and the smoke can only be taken in a figurative way. Since this can't be taken literally, and neither can Revelation 19:3, there seems little reason to take Revelation 14:11 literally either. As for the drinking of the wine of God's fury, an Old Testament prophetic verse, from an oracle against Edom, sheds further light on the interpretation of Revelation 14:

Just as you drank on my holy hill,
  so all the nations will drink continually;
they will drink and drink
  and be as if they had never been. (Obadiah 16)

The implication is that they drink themselves into oblivion, into nothingness. Then there's the second problematic verse, this time from chapter 20.

And the devil, who deceived them, was thrown into the lake of burning sulfur, where the beast and the false prophet had been thrown. They will be tormented day and night for ever and ever. (Revelation 20:10)

Since 20:15 says the *lost* will be thrown into the lake of fire, it is argued, their torment must also last for ever and ever. But can we safely move from the destruction of a beast and a false prophet and the devil to the destruction of sinners in hell, and take for granted they are analogous?

The beast and the false prophet are *corporate entities*, representing Rome the civil power and Rome the religious power. Can a government or a religion be tortured in fire? Not literally. Again, 20:15 doesn't explicitly say that sinners' torment is for ever and ever. Yet even if it did, I doubt such a figurative book as Revelation would be able to settle the fundamental question conclusively.

Death and Hades will also be destroyed in the fire, according to Revelation 20:14, but what does that mean except that they will come to an end? As in the case of the beast and the false prophet, it's difficult to conclude anything definite about the fate of sinners from this. The one definite piece of information we do have is the following:

> And each person was judged according to what he had done. Then death and Hades were thrown into the lake of fire. The lake of fire is the second death. If anyone's name was not found written in the book of life, he was thrown into the lake of fire. (Revelation 20:13b,14–15)

Could "the second death" be the final extinction of the individual? The first death is simply the death we'll all experience, unless Jesus returns while we're still alive. It's normal physical death. The second death, on the other hand, is the destruction mentioned in Matthew 10:28. There's no life, no consciousness, nothing at all after the second death. Isn't this the natural reading of the passage?

The Old Testament allusion in Revelation 20 is to Psalm 140:9-10. Let's take a look at Psalm 140 so we can be sure we are understanding Revelation correctly:

> Let the heads of those who surround me
>   be covered with the trouble their lips have caused.
> Let burning coals fall upon them;
>   may they be thrown into the fire,

into miry pits, never to rise.

"The trouble their lips have caused" implies that the punishment will fit, or be in proportion to, the crime. The limit is determined by the amount or nature of the "trouble" caused. Obviously the "trouble" isn't infinite, so it is unwarranted to assume the pain of the fire is infinite. This appears to be the Old Testament background of Revelation 20. Remember, the Old Testament is the key for understanding Revelation. In 404 verses, there are over 500 Old Testament references and allusions. That's why I always recommend people read the entire Bible before coming to any hard and fast conclusions about the last book of the Bible. Revelation 20:10, which deals with the devil, cannot be used to prove the duration in hell of the punishment of unforgiven sinners. Let's close the discussion of Revelation by returning to one of the final verses:

> And if anyone takes words away from this book of prophecy, God will take away from him his share in the tree of life and in the holy city, which are described in this book. (Revelation 22:19)

The "tree of life" gave immortality, according to the Genesis account. Even true Christians can *lose* their immortality, which is a God-given blessing, if they tamper with the word of God. But if the traditional view is right, it's impossible for anyone to lose his immortality, which is considered innate and automatic.

Summing up on Revelation, neither of the problematic verses conclusively teaches that people will be tortured forever in hell. It simply isn't there.

Summary: Initial objections

I've taken all this time to answer the most common objections in order to show that the terminal view *is* a viable interpretation. Though the bulk of the positive evidence for this view is forthcoming, it will be nowhere near as persuasive to someone who has already made up his mind on the interpretational possibilities. We saw that Jesus' words in Mark 9, often presumed to back the traditional view, actually strongly support the *terminal view*. Matthew 25, on the other hand, though seeming at first to support the *traditional view* (and without other passages to clarify, it appears to do so decisively), is inconclusive because of the ambiguity of "eternal." There are good reasons to understand "eternal" in the second, also biblically common, sense. This fits in excellently with Jesus' words in Matthew 10:28: "Rather, be afraid of the One who can destroy both soul and body in hell."

As for Revelation, interpreted by many to support the traditional view incontrovertibly, it does nothing of the kind. Revelation 14 draws on Old Testament imagery where the image of eternal burning cannot possibly be construed to be "eternal" in the literal, traditional sense. The same can be said of Revelation 20.

The traditional view, if it is true, must base itself on clear, non-ambiguous passages of scripture. However, the most compelling passages marshaled to support it are all somewhere between ambiguous and detrimental to the view!

II. THE TERMINAL POSITION ON HEAVEN & HELL

The terminal view finds support in both Old and New Testaments, which teach the same on the judgment day, the mortality of the soul, heaven as the reward for the righteous and hell culminating in annihilation as the punishment for the wicked.

A. Support from the Old Testament
1. There will be a Judgment Day.

This may not come as a shock to most, but just to set the record straight let's review the biblical teaching in the Old Testament.

And God will call the past to account...
I thought in my heart,
"God will bring to judgment
    both the righteous and the wicked,
for there will be a time for every activity,
    a time for every deed." (Ecclesiastes 3:15,17)

Since not all right is rewarded nor all wrongs righted here in the earthly life, God will take care of things afterwards. Judgment Day involves a review of all actions, to be carried out when the time is right. See also Ecclesiastes 11:9.

Now all has been heard;
    here is the conclusion of the matter:
Fear God and keep his commandments,
    for this is the whole duty of man.
For God will bring every deed into judgment,
    including every hidden thing,
    whether it is good or evil. (Ecclesiastes 12:13–14)

Will he not repay each person according to what he has done? (Proverbs 24:12)

This last verse is the one Paul uses in his discussion of judgment in Romans 2:6. He appeals to the authority of the Old Testament as New Testament writers constantly did. It would be hard to appeal to the Old Testament if it taught inaccurately on these matters.

One thing God has spoken,
    two things have I heard:

that you, O God, are strong,
   and that you, O Lord, are loving;
Surely you will reward each person
   according to what he has done. (Psalm 62:11–12)

These things you have done and I kept silent;
   you thought I was altogether like you.
But I will rebuke you
   and accuse you to your face. (Psalm 50:21)

Exactly when will this rebuke occur? The storms of life (Matthew 7:25) don't always do the trick, and it seems God is keeping silent for the time being. But he will speak, and there will be many surprised people at the judgment (Psalm 73:17). Their face-to-face rebuke is pending. (Further evidence comes from Proverbs 11:19,21,23.)

Thus we see that the Old Testament teaches a time of judgment, with subsequent reward or punishment, in accordance with one's deeds. Moreover, this teaching isn't limited to the wisdom literature or the prayers of the psalmists. Just like the New Testament, the Old Testament teaches a comprehensive judgment (Genesis 18:25, Deuteronomy 32:35-36, Hebrews 10:30, Romans 12:19).

2. Man is mortal.

The doctrine of man's mortality is well established in the Old Testament, but the traditional or orthodox view is that the human soul is eternal. The scriptures, however, do not contain the doctrine of the immortal soul.

Often it is said that Old Testament writers taught man's mortality (i.e., no "eternal life") because of their limited knowledge about the afterlife. There is another possibility, however: that the immortality of the soul is a false assumption, unsupported by the

Bible. The lack of support in the Old Testament in this case doesn't need to be explained away; it is to be expected.

The surprising thing is that the Old Testament isn't simply silent on the subject. There's a definite "Old Testament" teaching. I put that in quotation marks because it's not really *only* an Old Testament teaching; it's a *Bible* teaching. (In the same way, it would be misleading to say that God's goodness is an Old Testament teaching, since the New Testament teaches exactly the same thing.) The real question is, "What does the *Bible* teach?"

In the Old Testament we read of *Sheol* as the abode of the dead, rendered "hell" in older translations, yet in modern English translations we do not find the word "hell" anywhere in the Old Testament. Yet this shouldn't be taken to mean hell is only a New Testament concept. Quite the contrary. Let us return to Psalm 140:

> Let the heads of those who surround me
>> be covered with the trouble their lips have caused.
>
> Let burning coals fall on them;
>> may they be thrown into the fire,
>> into miry pits, never to rise. (Psalm 140:9–10).

The wicked will be thrown into the fire. They will be swallowed up. They will be "consumed." The lake of fire is foreshadowed in the Old Testament. (Revelation 20 appropriately borrows and adapts this feature in its description of the punishment of the wicked, particularly the opponents of the Christians in the Roman Empire. These enemies of the faith were also slanderous persecutors, just like David's enemies in Psalm 140:11.)

Just as the doctrine of the mortality of the soul has not found wide acceptance within Christendom, so it is within Islam. Interestingly, the *Qur'an* too seems to allow for an end to the torment of the wicked in hell:

> As to the duration of heaven and hell, all Muslims agree that the state of
> bliss in heaven is eternal. The Qur'an itself assures believers of the eter-
> nality of heaven (3.198, 4.57, 50.34, 25.15). But there is no unanimous
> agreement as to the duration of the lost in hell. The Qur'an speaks of the
> punishment and torment of eternity, and describes the fire and hell itself
> as eternal (10.52, 32.14, 41.28, 43.74). The majority of orthodox Muslims
> accept the eternality of hell based on this testimony. On the other hand,
> based on such passages as 78.23, 11.107, and 6.128, which indicate the
> damned will remain in fire for a long time or will be there as long as God
> wills, many contemporary Muslims believe that the Qur'an leaves open
> the possibility that the punishment of hell will not last forever.

3. The saved will be with God in heaven eternally.

According to the Old Testament, we'll be with God "for
ever and ever," enjoying "eternal pleasures at [his] right hand"
(Psalm 21:4; 16:11). Nor is there any hint that the reward is re-
stricted to a limited period of time.

> Therefore my heart is glad and my tongue rejoices;
> 　my body also will rest secure,
> because you will not abandon me to the grave,
> 　nor will you let your Holy One see decay.
> You have made known to me the path of life;
> 　you will fill me with joy in your presence,
> with eternal pleasures at your right hand. (Psalm 16:9–11)

> And I—in righteousness I will see your face;
> when I awake, I will be satisfied with seeing your likeness. (Psalm 17:15)

While it is true that the notion of heaven was not developed in the Old Testament period, it would be false to claim heaven is exclusively a New Testament concept.

4. The wicked will be punished with fire.

As with the previous doctrine, the punishment of the wicked by fire is not as elaborately or explicitly taught in the Old Testament as in the New Testament, but, once again, it is intimated. Psalm 21:9, which appears in the next sub-section, is one example of a "fire" passage, as is the following:

Fire goes before him
and consumes his foes on every side. (Psalm 97:3)

Or take this passage from the prophets:

See, the Name of the LORD comes from afar,
with burning anger and dense clouds of smoke;
his lips are full of wrath, and his tongue is a consuming fire...
The LORD will cause men to hear his majestic voice
and will make them see his arm coming down
with raging anger and consuming fire,
with cloudburst, thunderstorm and hail.
The voice of the LORD will shatter Assyria;
with his scepter he will strike them down.
Every stroke the LORD lays on them with his punishing rod
will be to the music of tambourines and harps,
as he fights them in battle with the blows of his arm.
Topheth has long been prepared;
it has been made ready for the king.
Its fire pit has been made deep and wide,
with an abundance of fire and wood;
the breath of the LORD,

> like a stream of burning sulfur,
>> sets it ablaze. (Isaiah 30:27,30–33)

Fire is the most common metaphor for judgment and punishment in the Bible, and the Old Testament is no exception.

5. The wicked will be destroyed, not just tormented forever.

If this proposition is true, then either we must rely upon the New Testament alone for the concept of unending conscious torment or admit that the traditional view is the product of human theology. That in itself wouldn't be surprising, considering the many doctrines that began to be spawned at the very time the New Testament was being written. The issue, however, must be settled from the Bible itself.

> Your hand will lay hold on all your enemies;
>> your right hand will seize your foes.
> At the time of your appearing
>> you will make them like a fiery furnace.
> In his wrath the LORD will swallow them up,
>> and his fire will consume them. (Psalm 21:8–9)

This portion of scripture says that the wicked will be *consumed*. When you consume your dinner, what's left? Nothing. See also Psalm 59:13. How long does the consumption last? Until they are no more. The effect, however, is eternal; there isn't the slightest chance of it ever being reversed. They will cease to *exist*.

> Those who are far from you will perish;
>> you destroy all who are unfaithful to you. (Psalm 73:27)

> The senseless man does not know,
>> fools do not understand,

that though the wicked spring up like grass
   and all evildoers flourish,
they will be forever destroyed. (Psalm 92:6–7)

The wicked man will see and be vexed,
   he will gnash his teeth and waste away;
   the longings of the wicked will come to nothing. (Psalm 112:10)

Notice the progression in this last Psalm. The wicked man proceeds along this path:

Vexed →gnashing teeth →wasting away.

In the Bible, gnashing of teeth is a sign of *anger, not agony.* The wicked man doesn't gnash his teeth forever; he ultimately wastes away. We've been conditioned to think of gnashing of teeth as the involuntary response of souls in torment, whereas actually it is the proud and angry response of those who refuse to humble themselves before God. In Psalm 37 it isn't possible to take "gnashing" as a pitiful act of agonized torture. Here it's the proud and willful expression of scorn by a wicked person towards the good:

The wicked plot against the righteous
   and gnash their teeth at them;
but the LORD laughs at the wicked,
   for he knows their day is coming. (Psalm 37:12–13)

Taking the verse in context, the gnashing is going on *before* judgment day. The common understanding of gnashing as a response to torment is incorrect. In the Bible it's a sign of *anger, not agony.* Recall how the Jews gnashed their teeth at Stephen before stoning him (Acts 7:54).

God's wrath runs its course (Isaiah 57:16 and Psalm 103:9). Although it could last infinitely long, if that were God's will, the Scriptures show that his punitive action in hell is *limited* in duration. There's *logically* a limit to God's anger. Logically, because the punishment for sin is in proportion to the sin itself. A finite quantity of sin doesn't require an infinite amount of punishment.

One final comment on the destruction of the wicked: *Spiritual* death isn't the same thing as *physical* death. Let's not be confused. The wages of sin is physical death, according to Romans 5. Through Adam sin and death entered the world. But there's a further kind of death: spiritual death. (In one sense, of course, as non-Christians we were dead spiritually [Ephesians 2], but this is a figurative sense.)

The spirit of man dies when God destroys both soul and body in hell (Matthew 10:28). Sooner or later all men die physically. But to perish spiritually (Luke 13:5)—that is a much more frightful thing. The point is that, just as physical death means the end of life in the physical body, so spiritual death means the end of life as spiritual beings. We are all created as spiritual beings, so when our spiritual life ends we cease to exist.

You may also want to consult these verses on the ultimate destruction of the wicked: Psalm 9:5, 37:20, 37:37-38, 68:2, 104:35, Proverbs 12:7, 21:28, 24:19-20.

Conclusions: The Old Testament

Before you study *closely* the Old Testament teaching about the afterlife, it may seem the Old Testament is silent about heaven, hell, and the traditionally accepted Christian picture. In fact, it is not silent. It only seems silent because it gives no support to the accepted view. The Old Testament, once again, isn't silent about the end of the wicked. It's only silent as to the view we would expect to find.

Before moving on to the New Testament teachings, let me state one of the most surprising conclusions I've come to in my study:

The Old and the New Testament teach substantially the same things about heaven and hell.

The Old and New Testament are in harmony. This shows the organic unity and harmony of the scriptures. The Old was the Bible for the early Christians, and the teachings of the New are a continuation of and complement to the teachings of the Old Testament.

B. Support from the New Testament

Summarizing the Old Testament teaching on the subject:

1. Judgment Day with two alternatives.
2. Man is mortal. Immortality isn't innate, it's a reward.
3. The saved will be with God in heaven eternally.
4. The wicked will be punished with fire.
5. This punishment ends in *destruction*, not eternal torment.

Most of us are so much more familiar with the New Testament teaching on these matters that fewer verses are needed to substantiate the basic points than for the discussion of the Old Testament and afterlife. This is especially the case for sections 1, 3 and 4. The new view is brought out most clearly in sections 2 and 5.

1. Judgment Day

Jesus reaffirmed the Old Testament doctrine of the day of judgment.

"Do not be amazed at this, for a time is coming when all who are in their graves will hear his voice and come out—those who have done good will rise to live, and those who have done evil will rise to be condemned" (John 5:28–29).

See also Matthew 25. Purgatory is ruled out of court, as it lacks supporting scripture. The New Testament teaches but two alternatives.

2. Man is mortal, immortality is a gift.

The New Testament teaching of the mortality of the soul is identical to the Old Testament teaching, a consistent thread of doctrine from Genesis onward.

> "For just as the Father raises the dead and gives them life, even so the Son gives life to whom he is pleased to give it." (John 5:21)

> "You [the Jews] reject it and do not consider yourselves worthy of eternal life..." When the Gentiles heard this, they were glad and honored the word of the Lord; and all who were appointed for eternal life believed. (Acts 13:46b,48)

> To those who by perseverance in doing good seek glory, honor and immortality, he will give eternal life. (Romans 2:7)

Now we must admit that these are difficult verses to understand if we were born immortal. **Eternal life is conditional** (not for everybody) and positive. If we were *innately* immortal, then immortality wouldn't be conditional. And if one can be immortal in hell, then for most of humanity, immortality is the greatest imaginable *curse*. In the Bible immortality is presented *as a blessing*:

> For the wages of sin is death, but the gift of God is eternal life in Christ Jesus our Lord. (Romans 6:23)

> I declare to you, brothers, that flesh and blood cannot inherit the kingdom of God, nor does the perishable inherit the imperishable...For

the perishable must clothe itself with the imperishable, and the mortal with immortality. (1 Corinthians 15:50,53)

Mortality *can* yield to immortality. This is awesome! But is it an automatic change happening to every human soul at judgment, regardless of his or her spiritual standing before God? Not at all. This inheriting of immortality is a positive thing, sung to the tune of victory:

When the perishable has been clothed with the imperishable, and the mortal with immortality, then the saying that is written will come true: "Death has been swallowed up in victory." (1 Corinthians 15:54)

...the hope of eternal life, which God, who does not lie, promised before the beginning of time. (Titus 1:2)

Now if this is our *hope* (eternal life), do we possess it *innately*, whether or not we follow Christ? Romans 8 and some clear thinking elucidate the matter:

But hope that is seen is no hope at all. Who hopes for what he already has? (Romans 8:24b)

If we already had eternal life, we wouldn't need to hope for it. Yet not until the last trumpet will eternal life unconditionally be ours. Eternal life is a reward for the saved—and for the saved only. This is also the teaching of Jude and Revelation:

Keep yourselves in God's love as you wait for the mercy of our Lord Jesus Christ to bring you to eternal life. (Jude 21)

Yes, we begin to receive eternal life in baptism, but in another sense the victory isn't clenched till we've died faithful. By that time it's impossible to fall away and forfeit the enormous gift we've received. Eternal life will be our reward.

> And if anyone takes words away from this book of prophecy, God will take away from him his share in the tree of life. (Revelation 22:19)

It is indeed possible to lose our share in the tree of life. If that happened, we would certainly not live forever. Once again, check it out in Genesis:

> "[The man] must not be allowed to reach out his hand and take also from the tree of life and eat, and live forever." (Genesis 3:22b)

Just as in the Old Testament, the New Testament teaches immortality is a reward from God, a reward only for the faithful. The traditional idea of *unending conscious torment and innate immortality* is severely at odds with the Bible.

Incidentally, several early writers affirmed the eternal torment view: Justin, Jerome, and Augustine, to mention a few of the big names. Yet several of the early church fathers also advocated infant baptism, apocryphal writings, even the priesthood. The point is that regardless of what leading intellectuals taught, the Bible and the Bible only is authoritative in settling biblical questions.

3. The saved will be with God in heaven.

You knew that already, but just to be encouraging, remember what Paul wrote:

> And so we will be with the Lord forever. (1 Thessalonians 4:17)

No one contests this, the supporting scriptures are ample, and this paper is really a new view of hell, not heaven, so let's move on.

4. The wicked will be punished with fire.

The Old Testament teaching is repeated in the New:

But for those who are self-seeking and reject the truth and follow evil, there will be wrath and anger. (Romans 2:8)

What kind of wrath and anger? In Mark 9 Jesus, much to the chagrin of modern "churchianity" and its professional clergy, speaks at length about hell:

"If your hand causes you to sin, cut it off. It is better for you to enter life maimed than with two hands to go into hell, where the fire never goes out. And if your foot causes you to sin, cut it off. It is better for you to enter life crippled than to have two feet and be thrown into hell. And if your eye causes you to sin, pluck it out. It is better for you to enter the kingdom of God with one eye than to have two eyes and be thrown into hell, where 'their worm does not die, and the fire is not quenched.' Everyone will be salted with fire." (Mark 9:43–49)

Like the Old Testament, the New Testament says the wicked are thrown into the fire. Whether the fire is literal or not is another matter. "Blackest darkness" (2 Peter 2:17, Jude 13) cannot *literally* describe a (presumably bright) lake of fire. In my opinion, both are metaphors, images. Not to say that hell will be less terrible than a lake of fire. Rather, the appropriate image of fire, fraught with overtones of destruction, judgment, holiness, and cleansing, gets us thinking the right way about hell. The reality to which a symbol points is never less real than the symbol itself; if a fiery lake is a symbol, we can be assured that hell is in reality far worse.

Interestingly, only Jesus and his brother James *explicitly* mention the burning fire of *Gehenna* (hell). Paul never explicitly mentions it, yet he gave the leaders of the church at Ephesus the "full counsel" (Acts 20:27). Draw your own conclusion. Before we discuss the fire's *duration*, let's move on to the final element in New Testament teaching on the afterlife.

5. The punishment ends in destruction.

In Luke 13:5 we read that unless we repent we "will all perish." But what does it mean to perish? In its basic sense the word carries no sense at all of continued existence or consciousness. The Latin word *perire*, which gives us our English word perish, means "to pass away, come to nothing, lose one's life." The Oxford English Dictionary gives this definition:

To come to an untimely end; to suffer destruction; to lose its life.

An end implies nothing further; destruction means annihilation, loss of life precludes eternal life. We know what the word *perish* means, but our understanding of Luke 13 has been determined by the Catholic Church, not by standard English usage.

In fact the definition of *perish* changed in late *Middle English* (around 1300). The later, modified meaning, according to the Oxford entry, was: "To incur spiritual death; to suffer moral ruin." But this isn't the original meaning of the word, which was redefined by the medieval church. We are all too familiar with the confusion caused by the *later* definition of the word *baptisma* (baptism).

Try to set aside the traditional view, at least for the time being. Ask Dante to wait outside the door till we've finished scouring the scriptures.

Matthew 7:13 tells us:

"Enter through the narrow gate. For wide is the gate and broad is the road that leads to destruction, and many enter through it."

Where does the broad road lead? To eternal torment? No, to *destruction*. This is more like the unthinking buffalo herd stampeding over the edge of the cliff than the masses falling into the hands of Lucifer's torturers.

Hebrews 10:26-27 says,

If we deliberately keep on sinning after we have received the knowledge of the truth, no sacrifice for sins is left, but only a fearful expectation of judgment and of raging fire that will consume the enemies of God.

The fire of God's wrath ("raging") will totally *consume* God's enemies. That requires some time. Consumption may be slow or it may be fast, but it isn't instantaneous. As Jesus described opposite destinies in Luke 16, the rich man wasn't finished yet.

To illustrate, if acid *consumes* an object, how much is left? None of it, if it's really consumed, and not just corroded. Consumption is total by definition. It's the same with eating. Once you consume your food, it's gone. Chew, swallow, digest, but once you've done that it's gone.

But we are not of those who shrink back and are destroyed, but of those who believe and are saved. (Hebrews 10:39)

If we shrink back we'll be punished. But the truth is that we'll also be *destroyed*. The passage says nothing of a sort of "figurative" destruction. Destruction is destruction.

> Then death and Hades were thrown into the lake of fire. The lake of fire is
> the second death. If anyone's name was not found in the book of life, he
> was thrown into the lake of fire. (Revelation 20:14-15)

To understand the "second" death, begin by asking what the first
one is. Of course it's physical death. The second one is the spiritual
capital punishment administered by God:

> "Rather, be afraid of the One who can destroy both soul and body in hell."
> (Matthew 10:28)

God can *destroy* our souls. This passage isn't talking about Satan.
He is one of those who will be cast into hell (Revelation 20:10).
When God destroys a soul, there will be nothing left. After that
point the soul will no more survive than our physical body will
survive. The soul of man is most emphatically *not* eternal. Not according to Jesus.

      2 Peter 2:6 says,

> [I]f he condemned the cities of Sodom and Gomorrah by burning them
> to ashes, and made them an example of what is going to happen to the
> ungodly..."

What *is* going to happen to the ungodly? They are going to go to
hell. The punishment of hell is not under dispute. Hell is biblical,
real, and horrible. The issue is: What is the nature of the punishment? And this passage says that Sodom and Gomorrah, which
were burnt to ashes, are an example of what will happen to the
ungodly. So if the traditional view is correct, why aren't these cities *still* burning?

> They are like brute beasts, creatures of instinct, born only to be caught and destroyed, and like beasts they too will perish. (2 Peter 2:12b)

> By the same word the present heavens and earth are reserved for fire, being kept for the day of judgment and destruction of ungodly men. (2 Peter 3:7)

Destruction is the order of the day, not eternal conscious torment. Yet some will experience a longer punishment than others, as Luke 12 makes clear:

> "That servant who knows his master's will and does not get ready or does not do what his master wants will be beaten with many blows. But the one who does not know and does things deserving punishment will be beaten with few blows. From everyone who has been given much, much will be demanded; and from the one who has been entrusted with much, much more will be asked." (Luke 12:47–48)

Responsibility is proportional, and judgment is based on ability and knowledge. This isn't just logical, it's biblical.

Jesus' analogy makes an assumption about time. If it should be taken literally, some were going to receive more blows than others. Which takes longer, few blows or many? Many, of course. In other words, some punishments will last longer than others. That's the implication of the text. So the length of the punishment is proportional to the amount of guilt, or the level of responsibility the individual has failed to live up to.

Another implication is that the punishment will eventually end. This means that whether it is a million years or forever—however hard psychologically for us to grasp—does actually make a difference. We are not splitting hairs here. In mathematics class, students are not allowed to "round up" really large numbers to infinity. The difference, in fact, between any number, however large, and infinity is *infinity*. One is *limited*, the other is *infinite*. That is precisely the point of this article: that the punishment of hell runs its course.

Summary so far

Both Old Testament and New Testament teach the same: a punishment for the wicked that begins in torment and ends in destruction. Once again, consider the paradigm laid out at the beginning of the article:

Traditional view:	(Infinite) corporal punishment
Annihilationist view:	Capital punishment
Terminal view:	Corporal + capital punishment

III. RELATED QUESTIONS

Many protests have been leveled against this view, and they're not to be taken lightly. As Proverbs 18:17 says, "The first to present his case seems right, till another comes forward and questions him." A good theory must be able to stand the test of criticism.

Yet are the objections really weighty enough to support the traditional view and overthrow this one? Not at all, as we shall see.

A. If the new view is right, why didn't Jesus ever correct the traditional view?

Quite simply because the "traditional" view may not have ever really caught on till well after Jesus' time. We've assumed Jesus supported the traditional view through default. (He never tried to correct the common misunderstanding.) But what makes us so

sure first-century Jews held to eternal punishment in the traditional sense?

They hadn't gotten the idea from the Old Testament. Neither the Old or the New Testament teaches eternal torment. Like
me, you probably thought it was somewhere in there, right? (Which
verse? I haven't been able to find it.) Plato, four centuries earlier,
had taught the immortality of the soul, but his influence was little
felt in New Testament times. And the first time the Apocrypha,
written shortly before and after the first century, speaks of eternal
torment is Judith 16:17. So where did Jesus' contemporaries sup-
posedly get the view of infinite hell?

Moreover, are we sure there was a consensus in Jesus'
day? Why would Jesus have attempted to correct the prevailing
view if there was no unified view in his day? (It would certainly be
misleading to claim there's only one view on the afterlife in today's
religious world.)

Yet even if the majority of Jews in Jesus' day *did* believe in
the later Catholic view, and even if for his own reasons Jesus made
no attempt to enlighten them, that's irrelevant, ultimately, as far
as we're concerned. The question about hell is a biblical question,
and its answer needs to be derived, ultimately, from the Bible.

Views about Jesus' reasons for addressing or not addressing various conceptions floating around in his day are bound to be
highly speculative.

B. Luke 16: The rich man

This turns out not to be much of an objection, since the
passage never says the rich man would be in Hades forever, only
that "those who want to go from here to you cannot, nor can anyone
cross over from there to us" (Luke 16:26). We may *assume* he would
be there forever, and certainly many have shuddered to think of
their loved ones in hell "for eternity." But the traditional torment

interpretation has been read into the text—which, honestly, allows either view.

A couple of notes are in order about this passage. First, the NIV has mistranslated Hades, the waiting place in the underworld, as "hell." Yet this is not the Greek word for hell (*Gehenna*). Second, you may wonder, why is someone in the fire if this isn't hell? Jesus has adapted a common story—about a rich man and a poor man, whose roles are reversed in the next world—to make his point. We are not obligated to take the passage literally. Yet even if we do, the dread of the judgment day—still future—was a sort of punishment itself. Even the demons dreaded torment in advance of the judgment (Matthew 8:29). And in the early church arose the belief that the damned could feel the heat of the lake of fire even before their irrevocable sentence.

C. Galatians 1:9: Eternally condemned

The Greek words *anathema esto* strictly speaking do not read "let him be eternally condemned," but rather "let him be 'anathema.'" *Anathema* is the strongest possible curse, but no hint of eternal torment is inherent in the Greek. The NIV translators have opted for a more traditional translation of the Greek expression, which is fine, provided we haven't determined in advance what "eternally condemned" means.

Remember, eternal condemnation doesn't necessarily mean eternal torment, as we have seen, but rather an eternal sentence from which there will never be escape or appeal. So this isn't a case of mistranslation. As in the instance of Luke 16, we see how easy it is to read our position into the text. We read "eternally condemned" and think, "See—it says '*eternally* condemned.' Hell is eternal." Well, hell is eternal, but that's not the question. The question is what "eternal" means in this context, and what "eternal condemnation" means in the Bible.

If the verse had said, "Let him be *eternally* tormented," we would have a case for the traditional view. But it doesn't, and so we don't. Moreover, Galatians 6 teaches the opposite of the traditional view anyway:

> The one who sows to please his sinful nature [in Greek sarx, flesh], from that nature will reap destruction; the one who sows to please the Spirit, from the Spirit will reap eternal life. (Galatians 6:8)

Destruction is the end of the wicked, not eternal torment.

D. Matthew 5 and 18: Never getting out of prison

> "I tell you the truth, you will not get out until you have paid the last penny." (Matthew 5:26)

> "In his anger his master turned him over to the jailers to be tortured, until he should pay back all he owed. This is how my heavenly Father will treat each of you unless you forgive your brother from your heart." (Matthew 18:34–35)

Let's begin by honestly admitting that these passages are difficult to understand. Jesus could certainly mean that we *never* "pay" our way out, and thus remain in hell forever. On the other hand, he could also mean that we sooner or later *do* pay our way out. The passages allow either interpretation. But they absolutely do not *prove* the traditional view because they do not *prove* either view.

E. Luke 12:47: "That servant"

This passage says some will receive few blows, some many. Its application to hell seems clear and direct. Yet it has been objected that the proper context of Luke 12:47-48 rules out applying the principle to non-Christians. Take a look at the passage again:

> "That servant who knows his master's will and does not get ready or does not do what his master wants will be beaten with many blows. But the one who does not know and does things deserving punishment will be beaten with few blows. From everyone who has been given much, much will be demanded; and from the one who has been entrusted with much, much more will be asked." (Luke 12:47–48)

Peter had asked in verse 41, "Lord, are you telling this parable [about his return in judgment] to us, or to everyone?" In fact Jesus gave no direct answer to the question, instead discussing the master-servant relationship. Still, the passage does seem to apply to God's people more than to outsiders. But will God's delinquent people really be "beaten"? What about "no condemnation for those who are in Christ"? (Romans 8:1) And even if they were beaten (which in my mind is questionable theologically), then how much more would the principle suit non-Christians?

Moreover, the passage distinguishes between servants who know their master's will and those who don't. But don't all *Christians* essentially "know" their master's will? Those who know less, like non-Christians, are those "who do not know" (see also 2 Thessalonians 1:8).

The principle concerns knowledge and responsibility. Since this pertains to God's way of dealing with men, it seems unlikely that he would suspend the principle in the case of non-Christians. So while we can accept that the passage was originally spoken to the Twelve and applies to the servant people of God, it's untrue that the principle is invalid for the lost in general.

F. Daniel's three friends

[T]he fire had not harmed their bodies, nor was a hair of their heads singed; their robes were not scorched, and there was no smell of fire on them. (Daniel 3:27)

This passage too has been taken to illustrate or prove that God can keep sinners in the fire eternally. "See, the fire didn't kill them," it is pointed out. "The fire didn't destroy them—their physical bodies were somehow preserved." Yet by strict logic, this is actually an instance of God's *protection* from burning, hence a poor choice for the traditional view.

Once again, it's not disputed that God can do whatever he wants to. "Our God is in heaven; he does whatever pleases him" (Psalm 115:3). The point isn't what God can do, but what he *does*. Daniel's friends' circumstances give no assistance in supporting the traditional view.

G. What about the burning bush?

There the angel of the LORD appeared to him in flames of fire from within a bush. Moses saw that though the bush was on fire it did not burn up. (Exodus 3:2)

Does this passage prove that lost souls burn forever in hell? Naturally God has the ability to cause something to burn without burning up. Conceded. He's God, after all. But in this case the bush's burning was only temporary. Its combustion was assisted and prolonged by God, but not eternally.

IV. FINAL APPEAL

Well, the first has presented his case and the second has as well (Proverbs 18:17). How forceful do the objections seem to you now? I want to leave you with three questions:

1. Are you dissuaded from the terminal view because it takes more than one Bible scripture to explain the duration of hell? This is the case for many Bible teachings. To convincingly explain baptism or Jesus' divinity, it's helpful to use a number of verses. Do you think all this is exegetical gymnastics, or is it sound?

2. What does the Bible—not your minister, small group leader, church, commentary, or even your conscience or feelings—say about the subject? The Bible is our only arbiter and authority in settling the issue.

3. Is the alternative—the traditional view of hell/the immortality of the soul—really more convincing than the view here presented?

Of course you have to do your own homework, as a Berean of noble character (Acts 17:11). Re-read the paper, check the scriptures in context, think it through. Make your own decision. Finally, what will be different if we embrace this new understanding of judgment and hell? A number of things, but let's start with what will stay the same.

WHAT'S THE SAME

• Hell is still real, horrible, conscious, and irreversible.

- The terminal view is not "annihilationism," nor does it surrender the biblical teaching of the "raging fire which consumes the enemies of God."
- We still "sentence ourselves" by sin, failure to seek God, and rejecting the Savior.
- Evangelism is still imperative; no one goes to heaven apart from Jesus.
- There will still always be many who scoff at the concept of an authoritative and sovereign God who punishes.

WHAT'S DIFFERENT
- No one will "spend eternity" (infinitely) in hell. Punishment eventually terminates in destruction.
- Eternal life is a gift from God, not something automatic.
- The Old and New Testament square with each other.
- Many Christians will be relieved and enjoy the Christian life more than ever.

CHECK YOUR HEART

Don't let your feelings stop you from accepting this view, but on the other hand, don't let your feelings draw you into this view. Some of the implications are attractive, but we can't go around deciding doctrine based on our feelings.

My appeal to you, brothers and sisters, is to study the topic for yourself. (And not to rush to a hasty conclusion, nor to embrace this teaching because it appeals to you personally, but on biblical grounds first and foremost.)

Then we will be able to "leave the elementary teachings about Christ and go on to maturity, not laying again the foundation of...the resurrection of the dead, and eternal judgment. And God permitting, we will do so" (Hebrews 6:1-3).

Endnotes

Chapter One: After Death: Have We Got It All Wrong?

1. Other scripture references to the Valley of Ben Hinnom include: 2 Kgs 23:10; 2 Chr 28:3; 33:6; Jer 7:31; 19:2–6, 11–14; and 32:35, Is 66:24 (mentioned here); Mk 9:44-48.

2. The verbal form is *helan*.

3. R.W. Burchfield, ed., *The Oxford English Dictionary* (Oxford: Clarendon Press, 1986).

4. James H. Charlesworth, ed., *The Old Testament Pseudepigrapha*, vol. 1, *Apocalyptic Literature and Testaments* (Garden City, N.Y.: Doubleday, 1983–1985), 2 Enoch 8–10.

5. Edward William Fudge, *The Fire That Consumes: A Biblical and Historical Study of the Doctrine of Final Punishment, 3rd Edition* (Eugene, Oregon: Wipf & Stock, 2011).

Chapter Two: What the Early Christians Believed

1. Berçot, David, *A Dictionary of Early Christian Beliefs* (Peabody, Mass.: Hendrickson Publishers, Inc., 1998).

2. Alexander Roberts and James Donaldson, eds., *The Ante-Nicene Fathers: Translations of the Writings of the Fathers down to A.D. 325*, vol. 2, *Fathers of the Second Century: Hermas, Tatian, Athenagoras, Theophilus, and Clement of Alexandria (Entire)*, rev. ed. (1867; rev. and repr., A. Alexander Coxe, 1885; repr., Grand Rapids: WM.B. Eerdmans Publishing Company, 1953), 347.

3. Berçot, ___.

4. Roberts and Donaldson, eds., *Ante-Nicene Fathers*, vol. 1, *The Apostolic Fathers with Justin Martyr and Irenaeus*, 197.

5. Ibid., vol. 3, *Latin Christianity: Its Founder, Tertullian*, 52.

6. Ibid., vol. 5, *Fathers of the Third Century: Hippolytus, Cyprian, Caius, Novatian, Appendix*, 475.

7. Ibid., 1:239.

8. Ibid., 1:403.

9. Ibid., 1:560.

10. Ibid., 5:221.

11. Ibid., 5:221–222.

12. Ibid.

13. Ibid., 5:222.

14. Ibid., vol. 6, *Fathers of the Third Century: Gregory Thaumaturgus, Dionysius the Great, Julius Africanus, Anatolius and Minor Writers, Methodius, Arnobius*, 377.

15. Ibid., vol. 7, *Fathers of the Third and Fourth Centuries: Lactantius, Venantius, Asterius, Victorinus, Dionysius, Apostolic Teaching and Constitutions, Homily, and Liturgies*, 217.

16. Ibid., 3:557.

17. Ibid., 5:332.

Chapter Three: Problems and Objections

1. Ibid., 1:531.

2. M.G. Easton, ed., *Illustrated Bible Dictionary*, 3rd ed. (Thomas Nelson, 1879), s.vv. "Hades," "hell."

3. Orville J. Nate, ed., *Nave's Topical Bible* (Nashville, TN: Thomas Nelson Inc., Publishers, 1979).

4. W.E. Vine and Merrill F. Unger, eds., *Vine's Complete Expository Dictionary of Old and New Testament Words* (Nashville, TN: Thomas Nelson Publishers, 1984, 1996).

Chapter Four: End Times Theology: Armageddon, Antichrist, Apocalypse

1. For more on this, see an article at my website: Douglas Jacoby, "What is the Battle of Armageddon?," *International Teaching Ministry of Douglas Jacoby*, July 16, 2003, http://www.douglasjacoby.com/view _article.php?ID=2683.

2. For more on the book of Revelation and apocalyptic literature, try my audio series, *Revelation: Understanding the Book of Revelation*, available at my website, www.douglasjacoby.com.

3. Roberts and Donaldson, *Ante-Nicene Fathers*, vol. 2, *Fathers of the Second Century*, 67.

4. Ibid.,150.

5. Ibid., vol. 4, *Fathers of the Third Century: Tertullian, Part Fourth; Minucius Felix; Commodian; Origen, Parts First and Second*, 194.

6. Ibid., vol. 1, *Apostolic Fathers*, 528.

7. Ibid., vol. 3, *Latin Christianity*, 589.

8. Ibid., 590.

Chapter Five: Jesus' Descent into Hades

1. "The Apostles' Creed," Anglicans Online, last updated April 15, 2007, http://anglicansonline. org/basics/apostles.html.

2. "The Nicene Creed," Anglicans Online, last updated April 15, 2007, http://anglicansonline. org/basics/nicene.html.

We believe in one God,
the Father, the Almighty,
maker of heaven and earth,
of all that is, seen and unseen.
We believe in one Lord, Jesus Christ,
the only Son of God,
eternally begotten of the Father,
God from God, Light from Light,
true God from true God,
begotten, not made,
of one Being with the Father.
Through him all things were made.

For us and for our salvation
he came down from heaven:
by the power of the Holy Spirit
he became incarnate from the Virgin Mary,
and was made man.

For our sake he was crucified under Pontius Pilate;
he suffered death and was buried.
On the third day he rose again
in accordance with the Scriptures;
he ascended into heaven
and is seated at the right hand of the Father.

He will come again in glory to judge the living and the dead,
and his kingdom will have no end.
We believe in the Holy Spirit, the Lord, the giver of life,
who proceeds from the Father and the Son.
With the Father and the Son he is worshiped and glorified.
He has spoken through the Prophets.
We believe in one holy catholic and apostolic Church.
We acknowledge one baptism for the forgiveness of sins.
We look for the resurrection of the dead,
and the life of the world to come.
Amen.

Chapter Six: What Will We Do in Heaven?

1. Douglas Jacoby, *Genesis, Science & History*, (Spring Hill, TN: DPI,1996 and 2004).

Chapter Seven: What to Do with What You've Learned

1. F. LaGard Smith, *After Life: A Glimpse of Eternity Beyond Death's Door* (Nashville: Cotswold Publishing, 2003).

2. Douglas Jacoby, *What's the Truth About Heaven and Hell?* (Eugene, Oregon: Harvest House, 2013).

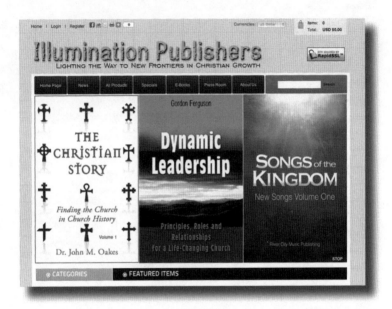

www.ipibooks.com